DATE DUE

DEMCO 38-297

ENTERED MAR 5 2002

The Papin Sisters

OXFORD STUDIES IN MODERN EUROPEAN CULTURE

GENERAL EDITORS

Elizabeth Fallaize, Robin Fiddian, and Katrin Kohl

Oxford Studies in Modern European Culture is a new series conceived as a response to the changing modes of study of European literature and culture in many universities. Designed to combine focus with breadth, each title in the series will present a range of texts or films in dialogue with their historical and cultural contexts—not simply as a reflection of history but engaged in a mediation with history, conceived in broad terms as cultural, social and political history. Flexible, interdisciplinary approaches are en-couraged together with the use of texts outside the traditional canon alongside more familiar works. In order to make the volumes accessible not only to students of modern languages but also to those studying the history or politics of modern Europe, all quotations are offered in both the original language and in English.

The Papin Sisters

Rachel Edwards and **Keith Reader**

OXFORD
UNIVERSITY PRESS

OXFORD

UNIVERSITY PRESS

Great Clarendon Street, Oxford OX2 6DP
Oxford University Press is a department of the University of Oxford.
It furthers the University's objective of excellence in research, scholarship,
and education by publishing worldwide in

Oxford New York

Athens Auckland Bangkok Bogotá Buenos Aires Cape Town
Chennai Dar es Salaam Delhi Florence Hong Kong Istanbul Karachi
Kolkata Kuala Lumpur Madrid Melbourne Mexico City Mumbai Nairobi
Paris São Paulo Shanghai Singapore Taipei Tokyo Toronto Warsaw
with associated companies in Berlin Ibadan

Oxford is a registered trade mark of Oxford University Press
in the UK and in certain other countries

Published in the United States
by Oxford University Press Inc., New York

British Library Cataloguing in Publication Data
Data available

Library of Congress Cataloging in Publication Data
Data available

ISBN   0-19-816010-0
ISBN   0-19-816011-9 (Pbk.)

1 3 5 7 9 10 8 6 4 2

Typeset in Utopia
by Best-set Typesetter Ltd., Hong Kong
Printed in Great Britain
on acid-free paper by
T.J. International Ltd.,
Padstow, Cornwall

Acknowledgements

The authors would like to thank the following: Malcolm Bowie, Lucille Cairns, Elizabeth Fallaize, Jill Forbes, Owen Heathcote, Paulette Houdyer, Alex Hughes, Ian Magedera, Eliane Meyer, Newcastle SML, North-Eastern Universities French, Ian Phillips-Kerr, Debbie Reisinger, Rocky Mountain Modern Languages Association, Society for French Studies, Twentieth-Century US French Studies Colloquium.

R. E.
K. R.

Contents

« Avant »

« Après »

Introduction

Reason was struck blind by the sisters, as if their plucking out of
their mistresses' eyes had metaphorically put out the eyes of their
interpreters.

(Ward Jouve 1998: 65)

No case in the annals of everyday crime in France has had so powerful and widespread an impact as that of the Papin sisters—Christine
and Léa, two housemaids who savagely slew their mistress and her
daughter in 1933. The 'everyday' is there in order to exclude crimes with
an explicitly political dimension to them—from Ravaillac's assassination
of Henri IV in 1610 through the Terror to the Occupation years. Among
what may rather cynically be described as the 'competition' might figure
the names of Lacenaire, the nineteenth-century fraudster and would-be
poet who allegedly served as inspiration for Raskolnikov in Dostoevsky's
Crime and Punishment; Marcel Petiot, the doctor who robbed and murdered at least twenty-seven Jews under the Occupation on the pretext
that he would help them to freedom; and Thierry Paulin, who with his
accomplice Jean-Thierry Mathurin killed twenty-one old ladies in north-
ern Paris between 1984 and 1987. Celebrated female killers include Violette Nozières, who poisoned her father and mother in the same year that
the Papins murdered their mistresses (the mother survived). Christine
Villemin was finally cleared in 1993 of the murder of her young son
more than eight years before, despite a luridly lyrical article by
Marguerite Duras strongly implying her guilt.

What a reading of that brief list will show is the importance of everyday, often domestic crime—what is known in French as the *fait divers*—
as a source for literature and film. That has been clear at least since
Balzac's Vautrin (supposedly based on the criminal-turned-police-chief
Vidocq) and Eugène Sue's best-selling *Les Mystères de Paris* in the 1840s,
and more so still in the age of cinema. Lacenaire is best known nowadays through the somewhat glamorized portrayal of him by Marcel
Herrand in Carné's *Les Enfants du paradis* (1945); Michel Serrault incarnated an expressionist view of Petiot in Christian de Chalonge's *Docteur
Petiot* (1990); the Paulin case is evoked in one of the main narrative

strands of Claire Denis's *J'ai pas sommeil* (1993); and Chabrol cast Isabelle Huppert in one of her best-known roles in *Violette Nozière* (*sic*) of 1978. Nor does the relationship between *fait divers* and literary or filmic text work in one direction only. Lacenaire almost certainly owes more of his fame to the combined efforts of Dostoevsky and Carné than to his real-life career, and Petiot's crimes, which might well otherwise have sunk into the kind of twilight zone that characterizes so much of *les années noires*, were so to speak introduced to a new generation by de Chalonge and Serrault.

If textual fecundity is at once guarantee and source of criminal noto-riety, then the Papins stand unchallenged at the head of the list. Their killings[1] inspired the Surrealists Éluard and Peret, were analysed in the article that first brought Jacques Lacan's work to a wider public, served as the basis for Genet's *Les Bonnes*, among the best known of post-war French plays, are evoked by both Beauvoir and Sartre, and have figured in one way or another in four feature films (including one by Chabrol— *La Cérémonie* of 1995), plus a documentary (see Afterword). Three full-length books—two 'factional' reconstructions, by Paulette Houdyer and Robert le Texier, and a psychoanalytical commentary by Françis Dupré— have also been consecrated to the case. Almost as we went to press a psy-choanalytic case-study of mother–daughter relationships—*Entre mère et fille: un ravage*, by Marie-Magdeleine Lessana—devoted a chapter to the affair. One major reason for our interest in the Papins was the extraordi-nary regularity of their cultural appearances over the sixty and more years since the killings. It is difficult to think of a case in British or American culture that goes back so far and continues to haunt textual representations to the same degree; why should this be so? To what extent does that unceasing fascination relate to what, following Benedict Anderson (Anderson 1983/1991), we may call France's 'imagined com-munity'? Even if such ambitious questions cannot be answered once and for all, an examination of the Papin case and of its multiple textual avatars, as well as being of great interest in its own right, will certainly help to bring them into focus.

We adopt throughout the book a 'cultural studies' approach—a vexed term, but one best understood here as the study of widely differing reproductions of the same event on an even footing. This is not to imply that a 'penny dreadful' such as Le Texier's *Les Soeurs Papin* is of equiva-lent value and interest to the theoretical developments adumbrated in Lacan's early article or to Genet's acknowledged theatrical masterpiece.

---

[1] It might be more appropriate to speak of 'killing', one single act involving four participants. Both forms will be found in our text, according to whether one form or the other seemed appropriate.

It is, rather, to contend that the very coexistence of these different types of textual reproduction—of an event itself accessible, by definition, only textually—is worthy of analysis and exploration, and that the bringing together of such texts may in itself be a socially, historically, and culturally illuminating enterprise. In so doing, we are mindful of the position in the cultural hierarchy we ourselves, and the likely readers of our book, occupy. To those who may feel that there is something distasteful about reviving—thus, in a sense, re-enacting—an act that destroyed its perpetrators and laid waste an entire family, we would respond that the Papin sisters' crime has, through the profuseness of its textual reproductions, already acquired a grisly kind of immortality, and that its very extravagance is what most cries out for analysis. Christine and Léa Papin, from the depths of their cultural deprivation, 'said' something when they so horribly murdered their mistresses. That something, if like the Lacanian 'real' it remains necessarily unsayable in its totality, continues to have a claim on our attention.

1 The Facts of the Case

The killings took place on the evening of 2 February 1933, at the Lancelin family home—6 rue Bruyère, in the city of Le Mans. That name generally evokes the celebrated 24-hour Grand Prix car race which takes place on the outskirts of the town, but Le Mans has other claims to fame than motor-racing and murder. It is the capital of the province of Maine, at the point where the Loire country shades off into Normandy and Brittany. It is a major railway junction on the westbound lines out of the Gare de Montparnasse (now only an hour from Paris by high-speed train) and an important centre of the car and food industries, as well as being a university city. Its population has very nearly doubled since the Papin sisters' day, when it clustered much more tightly around the old town centre—the cathedral of Saint-Julien and the *vieux Mans*, a handful of higgledy-piggledy medieval streets of wooden houses that still attract the tourists. The rue Bruyère is only a short distance from the old centre, an unremarkable street of terraced bourgeois houses.

Number 6 belonged in 1933 to M. René Lancelin, a retired solicitor who lived there with his wife and daughter Geneviève (there was another married daughter). The family seems to have led the kind of life that had characterized provincial France since Balzac's day. They had a fairly spacious house, had since 1927 employed the two Papin sisters as live-in maids, and shopped, dined, and card-played their tranquilly sociable way through life. M. Lancelin had spent the afternoon of 2 February playing bridge with friends, and returned home at about 6.30 p.m., expecting to find his wife and daughter there ready to join him for dinner at his brother-in-law's house. He was therefore extremely surprised to find the front door bolted against him and to get no response to his increasingly frantic knocking and ringing, the more so as a light could clearly be seen in the window of the maids' attic room. After two hours or so he went to the police station. Three policemen—two of whom bore the names of Ragot and Vérité[1]—managed to get into the house through a window at the back, and found Mme Lancelin and Geneviève lying

---

[1] These mean respectively 'morsel of gossip' and 'truth' in French. Still more curiously, another policeman involved with the case bore the name Deleuze, in common with the philosopher of schizophrenia whose best-known work is *L'Anti-Oedipe*.

across the landing, battered to death, their thighs and legs violently mutilated. More horrible still—and here surely resides what following Roland Barthes in *La Chambre claire* we might call the *punctum* of the case, that which gives it its particular and irreplaceable force—eyeballs lay on the stair-carpet, having been torn from the women with bare hands while they were still alive. That was, and so far as we have been able to tell remains to this day, unique in the whole of criminal history.

The horror of blinding and its evident link with castration, manifested in the Oedipus complex, were as we shall see to fuel much psychoanalytic interest in the case. This theme had been much in evidence in French culture a few years earlier, for 1928 had seen the appearance both of Buñuel and Dali's *Un chien andalou*, with its infamous opening sequence depicting the slitting open of an eye with a razor, and of Georges Bataille's *Histoire de l'oeil*, which culminates in an orgy at the height of which a priest's eye is torn from its socket.[2] Such thoughts would have been a very long way from the minds of the appalled policemen as they contemplated the bodies, before making their way upstairs, where they doubtless expected to find Christine and Léa likewise dead.

A locksmith was called and forced the door of the maids' room. Christine and Léa were side by side in bed, on the floor near them the hammer which had been used to batter Mme Lancelin and Geneviève to death. The sisters readily admitted that they were the killers, Christine claiming that it had been in self-defence. It was her words that were to give the killings the status of an act of class vengeance: 'J'aime mieux avoir eu la peau de nos patronnes que leur avoir laissé la nôtre.'[3] A bloodstained knife was found under Mme Lancelin's body, a battered pewter jug on the staircase—the other instruments of the crime. The sisters were immediately taken into custody. The following day's local newspaper, *La Sarthe du soir*, ran the story on its front page. Christine and Léa Papin's journey to gruesomely archetypal fame had begun.

The sisters' lives before the killings

Mistrust and fear of the 'lower orders', perceived as barely human and capable of the most hideous excesses, had long been a fairly widespread sentiment in France, particularly in reference to the Parisian 'mob'. The role played by the *sans-culottes* in the Revolution had left an enduring

---

[2] Buñuel and Dali were of course Spanish, but their film was shot in France.
[3] 'I'd rather have had our bosses' hides than for them to have had ours.'

trace in popular memory, and Louis Chevalier has admirably shown, in *Classes laborieuses et classes dangereuses*, how tenacious that perception of the Parisian proletariat and sub-proletariat was. Christine and Léa Papin, however, had in all probability never set foot in the capital, or indeed left their native department of the Sarthe, which has always had a somewhat unglamorous, not to say backward, reputation. This owes much to its location, sandwiched between the more touristically enticing regions of Normandy, Brittany, and Touraine, and about as close as it is possible to get to Paris while remaining within *la France profonde*—an expression only imperfectly rendered into English by 'deepest France'. *La France profonde* is by definition rural (but not coastal—it does not include Brittany, which qualifies handsomely on all other counts), impenetrable, and characterized by literal and metaphorical inbreeding, which was a crucial factor in the Papin case. It is an ideal location for the better-off class of Parisian intellectual to own a second home, though permanent residence there would be a species of purgatory. Provinces such as Auvergne and Burgundy spring most readily to mind when *la France profonde* is evoked, but the Sarthe, and the small province of Maine of which it forms part, qualified even more clearly in 1933 than today. Paulette Houdyer, author of the most widely sold book on the Papin case, has spoken of her profound attachment to the department where she was born and has always lived, and of her desire to explore the psychological complexities of the Papin sisters in part as a counterweight to sneering views of the Sarthe as a nest of yokels. Bookshops in Le Mans purvey glossaries of Sarthe idioms—an indication of cultural distance from the centre thrown all the more sharply into relief by the fact that the adjoining province of Touraine is classically that where the purest French is spoken.

La France profonde is no Arcadia—the inbreeding alone would ensure that—and has been the locale for some extremely gory crimes, real and imagined. Germaine Dulac's silent film *La Souriante Mme Beudet* (1922), set in Chartres which is the capital of a neighbouring department to the Sarthe, depicts the stifling tedium of life there and how it leads the heroine to fantasize about murdering her loathsomely self-satisfied husband. Bertrand Tavernier's film *Le Juge et l'assassin* (1976) is based on the real-life case of Joseph Vacher, a serial killer who operated in the eastern province of Franche-Comté during the Second Empire. Yet its working population has never inspired the same apprehension as those of the big cities—Paris, but also in different ways Marseille and Lyon. The humdrum tranquillity of its setting has tended to seem incompatible with such 'unnatural' violence as that shown by the Papin sisters. Yet we are about to see that that tranquillity and that violence were two sides of the same coin, so that the killing can in a sense be seen as the logical—but not predictable—consequence of what had gone before, the most spectacular of all the returns of the repressed of *la France profonde*.

Christine and Léa were the daughters of Gustave Papin and Clémence Derée (Paulette Houdyer gives the surname as Redré), who had married in 1901. At the time he worked in his father's cloth-mill, she in a seedsman's shop. Their first daughter, Emilia, was born in 1902. Gustave seems to have been of an amiable and accommodating disposition, Clémence more headstrong and flighty—there are suspicions that Gustave was not Emilia's father. Gustave found work in a sawmill in the village of Marigné, to which they moved in 1904, and in March of the following year Christine was born. It was at Clémence's insistence that she was brought up by Gustave's sister Isabelle; the marriage appears to have been a loveless one on her side at least and the children largely unwanted. Notwithstanding this, a third daughter, Léa, followed in September 1911, just before the marriage finally came to an end. Clémence claimed that Gustave had sexually molested Emilia, and the couple were divorced in May 1913. The two elder daughters were then placed in care in the Bon Pasteur orphanage and house of correction in Le Mans, shortly after which Léa, only 2 years old, went to live with an uncle. In 1918 Léa was boarded out in her turn and Emilia decided to enter a convent, which marked the effective end of relations with her family. So far as can be ascertained she was to pass the remainder of her days there.

Christine, unsurprisingly perhaps for one from so evidently dysfunctional a family background, expressed a wish to follow Emilia's example, which was indignantly rejected by her mother. The age of majority in France at the time was 21, up until which time parents had the deciding say on where their children lived, so Clémence's word was final. In 1920, Christine was placed as a maid with the Poirier family in Le Mans. Anybody who has experience of *chambres de bonne* in Paris—now often converted into studio flats, but no larger than they ever were—will tend to think of live-in domestic service as a painfully cramped and humble occupation, whose unattractiveness will be reinforced by Dr Louis Le Guillant's observations in his piece on the Papin case about the extraordinarily high rates of mental disturbance and suicide among that category (Le Guillant 1963: 911–12). For a woman as evidently unmaternal and (within the very limited means available to her) materialistic as Clémence, however, the lure of no longer having to fend for her daughters must have been considerable, while for Christine the escape from institutional surveillance and opportunity to learn a trade, however modest, might well have been tempting.

Her father kept well away from her after his abuse of Emilia, her elder sister safely behind the convent wall, her mother was at once indifferent and domineering, and Christine had only Léa to turn to for emotional sustenance. The extraordinary intensity of the emotional bond between the two sisters, without which their crime would have been inconceivable, derived from, as it nourished, their isolation in virtually all other respects. Maids were not particularly well paid, but their food and accommodation, however meagre, were provided; Christine and Léa turned out to have amassed surprisingly substantial savings, largely because they showed no interest in any kind of social or cultural life outside each other. Cafés, theatres, cinemas, dances held no attraction for them—maybe a reaction against their mother's extrovert lifestyle? Their only extravagance was clothes, presumably bought to be appreciated by themselves and each other. The sexual nature of their relationship completed the exclusive binding together of their dyad, ensuring that neither need want for or seek friends, family, or lover outside. That they were, as we shall see, to inspire the text in which Jacques Lacan first began to formulate the concept of the mirror-phase already begins to seem all too logical.

Christine and Léa first began working together some time after 1924, when Léa left the institution in which she had been a boarder. For the remainder of their free lives their greatest desire was to be employed (literally) under the same roof. It was in February 1927 that Christine was taken on by the Lancelins, to be joined by Léa two months later. It is significant that when first questioned by police after the killings Christine was to give the later date as that on which she had started work in the rue Bruyère. In October 1929 the sisters finally broke off relations with their mother. They were, at last, alone together.

There was virtually no verbal communication between the sisters and their employers. Mme Lancelin gave such domestic orders as were necessary, M. Lancelin and Geneviève uttering scarcely a word to Christine and Léa. Much was made of this, at the trial and in Lacan's article, but in the light of Le Guillant's observations, and the poignant quotation from a Spanish maidservant that he takes as his epigraph ('*Moi pas chien, moi humain*',[4] Le Guillant 1963: 868), it was probably far from unusual. The social, economic, and above all cultural gulf between the employing and employer classes was far too immense to be bridged by fleeting pleasantries or yield meaningful conversations. The representation of master–servant relationships at this time most likely to be familiar to

---

[4] 'I'm not a dog, I'm a human being.'

readers of this study is Jean Renoir's film *La Règle du jeu* (1939), in which the Marquise de la Chesnaye—named Christine—confides in her maid and the Marquis engages in good-natured banter with Marceau, the poacher briefly turned domestic servant. Renoir's characters, however, belong to the aristocracy (a luxurious Paris apartment, a country estate), and the relationship between the Marquis and Marceau makes sense only in the context of the film as a species of Bakhtinian carnival, in which the normal hierarchies of social relationships are inverted only to reassert themselves. In the world of the provincial bourgeoisie, altogether more financially and culturally restricted, the taciturn functionality of the relationship between the Lancelins and their maids might well have been the rule rather than the exception. It is significant that M. Lancelin's testimony situates the demise of any verbal communication between the sisters and their employers after the breach with their mother:

> Cette brouille avec la mère a aigri certainement le caractère des filles qui sont devenues aigres et taciturnes. Depuis cette époque, ni ma femme ni moi n'échangions de conversation avec elles en dehors du service. Elles étaient polies, nous sentions que les observations seraient mal reçues et comme notre service de maison était très bien fait, et ne donnait lieu à aucune critique, nous patientions.[5] (Dupré 1984: 142)

This was a curious thing to say, for two reasons. While the sisters' devouring absorption in each other would hardly have encouraged chit-chat at any time, with the Lancelins or anybody else, it clearly became exaggerated once they had severed links with their mother—the reverse, on a superficial reading at least, of what might have been expected. Furthermore, M. Lancelin's final sentence implies anything but an attitude of distant hauteur. 'Nous patientions' evokes—with hideous irony in view of what was to happen—the expectation, even the hope, of a change in the sisters' attitude, while 'nous sentions que les observations seraient mal reçues' no less ironically comes close to suggesting that the Papins exerted a bizarre kind of power over their employers. There are hints here, and elsewhere, of the emotional tensions and transferences that were to issue in the crime and have fed analysis and speculation ever since. The sisters habitually referred to Mme Lancelin—not, needless to say, to her face—as 'maman', and Louis Le Guillant has it that when their mother visited them after their verdict '[e]lles l'appelaient "Mme",

---

[5] 'The quarrel with their mother certainly embittered the sisters, who became gloomy and taciturn. Since then, neither my wife nor I had had any conversation with them outside their work. They were polite, and since we felt that they would take exception to any comment and they did their jobs in the house impeccably, we were patient.'

comme leur maîtresse'[6]—one of the many bizarre mirrorings with which as we shall see this case is riddled. In October 1928 Mme Lancelin is alleged to have compelled Léa to pick up a piece of paper she had dropped by pinching her arm until it bled. The precise balance between psychic and quasi-familial tensions on the one hand and 'normal' relations between dominant and dominated classes on the other is almost impossible to establish. What is certain is that by 2 February 1933 that balance had become a lethally unstable one.

The killings

The precise details of what happened that evening remain uncertain, for while neither sister ever attempted to deny guilt their accounts of who did what to whom varied significantly. The trigger for the attack was a blown fuse on the household iron, which Christine had collected from the repairers only the previous day. The cost of the repair had been deducted from the sisters' wages. This meant that Mme Lancelin and Geneviève returned to find the house in darkness, which, according to Christine, so angered the older woman that she attacked her. Christine's account (under questioning from Dupuy, the senior policeman on the case) is remarkable for its combined sang-froid and confusion:

> Voyant que Mme Lancelin allait se jeter sur moi, je lui ai sauté à la figure et je lui ai arraché les yeux avec mes doigts. Quand je dis que j'ai sauté sur Mme Lancelin, je me trompe, c'est sur Mlle Lancelin Geneviève que j'ai sauté et c'est à cette dernière que j'ai arraché les yeux. Pendant ce temps, ma soeur Léa a sauté sur Mme Lancelin et lui a arraché également les yeux. Quand nous avons eu fait cela, elles se sont allongées ou accroupies sur place; ensuite, je suis descendue précipitamment à la cuisine et suis allée chercher un marteau et un couteau de cuisine. Avec ces deux instruments, ma soeur et moi, nous nous sommes acharnées sur nos deux maîtresses. Nous avons frappé sur la tête à coups de marteau et nous avons taillardé le corps et les jambes avec le couteau. Nous avons également frappé avec un pot en étain qui était en place sur une petite table sur le palier, nous avons changé plusieurs fois les instruments de l'une à l'autre, c'est-à-dire que j'ai passé le marteau à ma soeur pour frapper et elle m'a passé le couteau. Nous avons fait la même chose pour le pot d'étain. Les victimes se sont mise [sic] à crier mais je ne me souviens pas qu'elles aient prononcé quelques paroles.[7] (Dupré 1984: 32)

---

[6] 'They called her "Madam", as if she were their mistress.'

[7] 'Seeing that Mme Lancelin was going to rush at me, I flung myself in her face and tore her eyes out with my fingers. When I say that I flung myself at Mme Lancelin, that's wrong; I flung myself

The police photographs reproduced in Dupré's book leave no room for doubt about the savagery of the assault. The women's legs were slashed, as Dupré points out, like meat being made ready for the oven, the blood that gushed from them mingling with the menstrual blood Geneviève was losing at the time. The Papin sisters also had their periods at the time of the killings, but were never again to do so afterwards—a contrary, and real-life, example of psychosomatic menstrual disorder to the heroines' aberrant menstruation in Marie Cardinal's *Les Mots pour le dire* or Marie Darieussecq's *Truismes*. Léa's account confirmed the details given by Christine, but was substantially more reticent. She was indeed to say, when first questioned: 'Pour moi, je suis sourde et muette'[8] (Dupré 1984: 164). Christine's statements, on the other hand, show an assumption rather than a mere acceptance of responsibility for the killings. 'Mon crime est assez grand pour que je dise ce qui est'[9] (Dupré 1984: 35) suggests an awareness, however unformed, that what she and her sister had done was an acting-out, in the most literal sense an *ex-pression*, a 'driving out', of something, or some variety of things, otherwise unsayable. The psychoanalytic interest taken in the case by Lacan and Dupré resides, we shall see, largely in this.

There had been an earlier intimation that all was not well with the sisters, in late August or early September 1931, when they had visited M. Le Feuvre, the mayor of Le Mans, making emotive but unfocused allegations of persecution. The town hall secretary had described them to the mayor as 'piquées' (= nutcases). Christine was subsequently to say that the purpose of their visit was to request the emancipation of Léa—still at the time a minor, though she had had full use of her earnings for two years—from her mother's tutelage. Eyewitness accounts, however, made no mention of this. Dupré argues that the mayor ('maire') was a homophonic surrogate for their mother ('mère'), from whom they were of course estranged—a view which suggests the intense emotional confusion and turmoil that were to erupt so dramatically two years afterwards.

---

at Mlle Geneviève Lancelin and tore out her eyes. While this was going on, my sister Léa leapt at Mme Lancelin and tore her eyes out. When we'd done that, they lay or squatted down on the spot; then I hurried down to the kitchen to get a hammer and a kitchen knife. With these two instruments my sister and I set about our two mistresses. We hit them over their heads with the hammer and slashed their bodies and legs with the knife. We also hit them with a little pewter jug which was on a little table on the landing, and we changed instruments several times—I handed the hammer to my sister and she handed me the knife. We did the same thing with the pewter jug. The victims began howling, but I don't remember their actually saying anything.'

[8] 'As for me, I am deaf and dumb.'   [9] 'My crime is great enough for me to tell the truth.'

What emerges fairly clearly from the different accounts given is that Christine, as the older and more intelligent of the two sisters, took the lead (she is quoted as having said: 'Je vais les massacrer'),[10] and that she and Léa agreed to share responsibility equally. They said to each other afterwards: 'En voilà du propre!'[11] before putting on their nightgowns and snuggling up in bed together to await the police. Incarcerated separately, they protested by refusing to eat or drink for a week. During the six months or so between their arrest and the trial, it was Christine whose behaviour was consistently the more bizarre. In July she had to be put into a straitjacket to prevent her from trying to tear out her own eyes. This led to a brief reunion with Léa shortly afterwards, at which she ecstatically removed her blouse and cried: 'Dis-moi oui! Dis-moi oui!'[12] (Certain journalistic accounts speak of her exposing her private parts and fondling her breasts, but there is no other evidence to support this.) It also seems to have been at this time that she said, when asked why she had removed Geneviève Lancelin's clothing: 'Je cherchais quelque chose dont la possession m'aurait rendue plus forte'[13] (Roudinesco 1993: 95). This might have been the phallus, in the symbolic sense in which Lacan uses the term—'[c]et inestimable objet de convoitise (celui qui n'existe pas, tout en encombrant la culotte de maman)'[14] (Saint-Drôme 1994: 140). (For a detailed exploration of the phallus in Lacan see Bowie 1991, ch. 5.) Whether or not we find a Lacanian reading acceptable, there is surely no doubt that the 'quelque chose' Christine was seeking had strong sexual overtones, for she had said in custody that in another life she had been, or was to be, her sister's husband. Yet the July outburst was less the consummation of that 'marriage' than a breach within it, for once Léa had been led away by the warders Christine abandoned her attempts to be permanently reunited with her. Her last mention of Léa's name occurs in a letter on 19 July. It is as if the killing and its aftermath had finally destroyed the couple of which they were such an intense affirmation.

The trial and contemporary reports on it

They nevertheless stood together, though not side by side (a policeman separated them), in the dock of the Le Mans Palais de Justice on 30

---

[10] 'I'm going to massacre them.'   [11] 'This is a pretty sight.'
[12] 'Tell me yes! Tell me yes!'
[13] 'I was looking for something whose possession would have made me stronger.'
[14] 'That priceless coveted object (the one which does not exist, even though it clutters up Mummy's pants).'

September. French legislation has always been fairly permissive in the matter of what can be said about suspects or accused in advance of a court's verdict, so that the guilt of the 'soeurs criminelles' had been bruited in the press from the moment of their arrest. An angry crowd massed outside the court, calling for the death penalty. This was still in force in France, as it was to remain until Mitterrand's accession to power in 1981, but no woman had been guillotined since 1887, though a journalist for *Candide* was to call for the Papins' beheading.

Inside the courtroom, forty journalists, mostly from Paris, were gathered. Their interest was less in the facts of the case, already widely known, than in the appearance and attitude of Christine and Léa. The notorious 'before' and 'after' photographs of the sisters—'before' dressed in their Sunday best, 'after' haggard and traumatized by the gaze of the police camera—have consistently fascinated writers on the case, notably Nicole Ward Jouve. *La Sarthe* described them in court as being 'comme des petites filles en classe alors que passe l'inspecteur', and commented on the distance between 'cette fille frêle (sc. Christine), toute ramassée dans son manteau' and 'la mégère surexcitée que nous vîmes le soir du crime'.[15] The banality, even the invisibility, of evil can of course be seen as an index of its presence quite as much as its most florid manifestations (something Dostoevsky among others knew only too well), so that the sisters' innocently cowed demeanour was—is—inevitably more complex than it seems. The distance on which *La Sarthe* comments could well be that between one schizophrenic manifestation and another, though we shall see that for Lacan it is paranoia, not schizophrenia, that provides the key to the killings.

Germaine Brière, the defence lawyer, observed: 'J'ai trouvé, au lieu de deux brutes, deux pauvres filles'[16]—a particularly poignant remark in its suggestion of a potential mother figure, what Melanie Klein would call a 'good breast', arriving only after the appalling violence its absence had brought about. The sisters' responsibility for their act was the main concern of a trial in which the facts of the case were scarcely in doubt. They answered questions in a whisper or not at all, suggesting no grudge against the Lancelins despite Christine's defiant formulation when arrested. The three official psychiatric experts gave it as their opinion that the sisters were guilty as charged and merited no mercy; one of them (Dr Truelle) had just been charged with the clinical examination of Violette Nozières. M. Houlière, the lawyer representing

---

[15] 'like little girls in school when the inspector comes round. . . . This frail girl, hunched up in her coat, and the overexcited shrew we saw on the night of the crime.'

[16] 'I found, instead of two brutes, two poor girls.'

M. Lancelin and his family, concluded his speech by saying: '. . . puisqu'elles se sont conduites en bêtes fauves, il faut les traiter en sauvages et en bêtes fauves.'[17]

This depressing revanchism, however, was not the only discourse on offer in the courtroom, or indeed outside. Dr Logre, described as a 'distinguished specialist in mental illness', was called as a witness for the defence, focusing on the sisters' mental state and in particular on the gulf between the shocking violence of the crime and its almost total lack of motive. *La Sarthe*'s report shows how many of the factors that have fascinated later writers about the case were at least touched upon in his speech—the element of sexual sadism, the sisters' ill-defined persecution complex (the town hall episode was cited as proof of this), what he termed 'l'extraordinaire duo moral que forment les deux soeurs, la personnalité de la jeune étant absolument annihilée par celle de l'aînée'[18] (Dupré 1984: 90). Logre concluded his speech with a plea for further investigation and psychiatric reports—hardly a realistic option in view of the interest and emotions generated by the trial, especially since the three court medical experts (who unlike him had been able to interview the sisters) steadfastly maintained the conclusion they had already reached.

Logre was interviewed after the trial by the 'true crime' magazine *Allo Police*, having meanwhile been able to speak with the sisters. This is the first mention I have been able to find of the incestuous nature of their relationship, effectively censored from the official reports on the case. Logre is unambiguous in his rejection of the Papins' statement that their affection was no more than a sisterly one, stating that:

> **Les soeurs Papin présentent toutes les apparences d'une affection anormale et amoureuse. Elles ne sortaient pas. On ne leur connaît nulle aventure sentimentale . . . Quand on les a séparées, à la prison, un désespoir insensé s'est manifesté chez Christine. Un amant éloigné d'une maîtresse adorée n'aurait pas eu de pires manifestations de douleur.**[19] (Dupré 1984: 92)

It is noteworthy that Logre imputes to Christine the 'masculine' role in the relationship, equating her with the male lover and Léa with the mistress in a manner that tallies with the stereotype of the male as more

---

[17] '. . . since they behaved like wild animals, they must be treated like savages and wild animals.'

[18] 'the extraordinary moral duo formed by the two sisters, in which the younger one's personality was absolutely annihilated by the older one's.'

[19] 'The Papin sisters give every appearance of having an abnormal relationship, that of lovers. They never went out. Neither was known to have any emotional adventures. When they were separated, in prison, Christine showed the most intense despair. A lover forcibly removed from his beloved mistress would not have shown greater signs of grief.'

active and assertive. This polarization is later invoked in support of his diagnosis of *folie à deux* (to be reprised by Lacan), for:

> **Quand un fou engendre une folie voisine, cas fréquent, il y a toujours un sujet actif et un sujet passif. C'est exactement le cas ici. Christine est active et ordonne, Léa est passive et obéit. Les experts n'ont pas noté cette observation.**[20] (Dupré 1984: 93)

The reservations we may well have about Logre's sweeping generalizations on *folie à deux* do not significantly detract from the thrust of his argument, which suggests that to equate the two sisters as identical partners in crime was to disregard the imbalance between them—an imbalance without that clearly betrayed an imbalance within. The sisters themselves, in their statements after arrest, initially seemed to endorse the 'official' view, stressing that they shared full and equal responsibility for the killings. As we have seen, however, this view was not to survive prolonged and repeated questioning, in the course of which Christine's dominance became ever more obvious. The Le Mans court clearly accepted this, as the different sentences handed down show, but not its possible implications concerning the sisters' sanity. Dupré points out that Logre's observations were published at the same time as Lacan's article, very shortly after the trial, which shows how rapidly what he calls the 'on-dit' of the case—the numerous discourses and reflections it inspired—came into play. What is remarkable is how many of the less condemnatory 'on-dits', such as that in *Allo Police*, figured in popular, non-intellectual publications.

Two further national publications—one a daily newspaper, the other an illustrated weekly—likewise go to illustrate this. For *L'Humanité*, published by the French Communist Party, the Papin sisters were victims not only of class, but—*avant la lettre*—of gender oppression. The issue of 28 September announced that: 'Ce procès ne devrait pas être celui des soeurs Papin toutes seules mais aussi celui de la sacrosainte famille bourgeoise, au sein de laquelle de se développe et fleurit quand ce n'est pas les pires turpitudes, la méchanceté et le mépris pour ceux qui gagnent leur vie à la servir.'[21] The issue of 29 September commented scathingly on the prosecuting counsel's description of the sisters as 'des

---

[20] 'When a mad person causes madness in somebody close to them—which is a common event—there is always an active and a passive subject. This is exactly what happens here. Christine is active and gives the orders, Léa is passive and obedient. The experts did not take this observation into account.'

[21] 'This trial should not be of the Papin sisters alone, but of the sacrosanct bourgeois family, in whose heart the worst depravities can flourish, to say nothing of malevolence and scorn for those who earn their living in that family's service.'

chiennes hargneuses qui mordent la main quand on ne les caresse plus!',
observing: 'Quant aux "caresses" dont parle Monsieur Riégert, les jeunes
exploitées des places bourgeoises savent ce que cela veut dire et qui [sic]
est une forme d'exploitation de plus.'[22] This article closes with a ringing
call to gendered political action ('Que des dizaines de milliers de "petites
bonnes," partie de la jeunesse exploitée, viennent aux côtés de leurs
soeurs des usines et des bureaux à l'action pour la défense de leurs
revendications, pour l'émancipation sociale').[23]

It is entirely predictable that a Communist Party publication should
have seen the sisters as victims of class oppression, which by virtue of
their condition they fairly obviously were. What is more surprising is the
awareness of their oppression as females, obvious enough to a contemporary readership but in those pre-feminist days rarely alluded to as
such. M. Lancelin's relations with the sisters were entirely proper,
but that is scarcely the issue. Gender oppression, in that Stalinist era,
was granted little or no space of its own in orthodox leftist discourse; it
was at best subservient to class oppression, at worst a bourgeois
diversion from it. One possible explanation for *L'Humanité*'s unusually
'modern' attitude is that this was the beginning of the period of *la main
tendue*—the policy of broadening alliances with non-marxist parties
and groupings that was to lead to the Popular Front government of
1936. The industrial working class was still seen as the mainspring of
revolution, but other social groups and categories were also welcome on
board, including domestic servants whose relative invisibility and all but
literal absorption into the lives of the bourgeoisie might hitherto have
consigned them to a minor place at best. It is interesting in this connection to note that Christine and Léa always refused to pay Social Security
contributions, preferring to rely on their cash savings—a mentality
supposedly characteristic of the peasantry, and indicative of how far
removed they and others like them were from the machinery of the
modern state that the Communist Party sought ambiguously to take over
or to smash.

Étienne Hervé, in the true-crime weekly *Détective*, also argued for
more understanding treatment of the sisters, on grounds of psychologi-
cally mitigating circumstances rather than class politics. *Détective* was a

---

[22] 'vicious bitches who bite the hand that no longer caresses them'... 'As for the "caresses" M.
Riégert mentions, the young women who are exploited in the bourgeoisie's service know only
too well what that means—it is yet one more form of exploitation.'

[23] 'May the tens of thousands of "ordinary maids", who form part of our exploited youth, join
their sisters in factories and offices in action for the defence of their demands and for social
emancipation.'

somewhat more complex publication than the label 'true-crime weekly' might suggest—associated with the left politically, incorporating 'reports on the great political-criminal affairs of the moment' (Rifkin 1993: 124) cheek by jowl with *faits divers*, making often sophisticated use of photo-montage. Hervé's article is less sensationalist than we might think from its title, 'L'Abattoir', pointing out that the two prosecution doctors had visited the sisters for only half an hour each, arguing for compassion on the grounds of the sisters' disturbed family background, and stressing, like Dr Logre, the need for more detailed expertise, preferably through a jury of medical specialists.

Nor were these left-wing Parisian publications the only ones to adopt a less vengeful and condemnatory tone. The weekly *Le Bonhomme sarthois*, whose title is scarcely the acme of metropolitan sophistication, had opined in February that the sisters did not appear in full possession of their faculties and were 'des névrosées qui, souvent, paraissent en état d'hypnose'.[24] On the day after the trial (1 October), the same publication proffered a view that strikingly complements *L'Humanité*'s, but this time from the side of the provincial bourgeoisie who for the Communist paper were the enemy: 'Personne ne peut se vanter de connaître à fond l'âme complexe des femmes et spécialement des servantes qui, chaque jour, circulent en silence autour de nous.'[25] Paranoia and the mirror-phase, we shall see, were to be fundamental to Lacan's work on the case in partic-ular, so that it seems appropriate that *Le Bonhomme sarthois* should both replicate the sisters' evident paranoia and mirror *L'Humanité*'s call to revolt. Christine and Léa appear less as pathological exceptions than as metonymic representatives of their class and gender, at once all too familiar and disconcertingly unknowable in their otherness—uncanny in the sense in which Freud uses the word when he defines it as 'that class of the frightening which leads back to what is known of old and long familiar' (Freud 1990: 340). The literary example Freud chooses to illus-trate his concept is that of the Sand-Man in one of Hoffmann's fairy stories—a character who tears out children's eyes.

Le Bonhomme sarthois's columnist Gros-René—a name redolent of peasant origins—also takes the opportunity to defend his depart-ment's capital against the slanderous remarks of (mostly Parisian) journalists. He denies that the inhabitants were in a frenzy at the time of the trial and that fire extinguishers were ready at the windows of the Palais de Justice, describing Le Mans as 'une ville calme, pondérée,

---

[24] 'neurotics who often appear to be under hypnosis.'
[25] 'Nobody can claim fundamental knowledge of the complex souls of women, and especially of the serving-women who each day make their way among us in silence.'

où personne ne s'emballe, même pour un procès sensationnel'. Such reactions, Gros-René goes on to say, would have been more likely in southern cities such as Toulouse, Marseille, or the much smaller Carpentras—*la France profonde* defending itself against the over-excitable Mediterranean, and protesting that 'il ne faut pas juger l'ensemble de la population sur deux démentes—car nous persistons à croire que les soeurs criminelles ne jouissaient pas de la plénitude de leurs facultés'[26] (*Le Bonhomme sarthois*, 8 Oct. 1933). Once more, the popular press of the time was to show greater acumen in judging the Papin sisters than the courts.

The verdict and its aftermath

Merciful judgments on women who killed were not uncommon in the France of the time. *La Sarthe* of 26 September 1933—only a few days before the Papin trial—records the case of a woman, also called Papin, who was spared after killing one of her thirteen children in a moment of despair, and mentions another woman's acquittal for the killing of her violent and drunken husband. The Papins, however, clearly constituted a case apart, and their jury's deliberations lasted a grand total of four minutes. Christine was condemned to be guillotined in the main square of Le Mans, Léa to ten years' hard labour. On hearing the verdict Christine fell to her knees in the dock.

Léa immediately appealed against her sentence, but Christine refused to do so. Throughout the month of November *Police-Magazine* ran a series of articles by Maurice Corien calling the sisters' sanity into question. Léa's appeal was rejected on 30 November, and Christine's sentence, despite her refusal to appeal, commuted by the President, Albert Lebrun, to hard labour for life on 22 January 1934, whereupon the sisters were transferred to prison in Rennes. Christine's mental condition steadily worsened; she persistently repeated that she was 'bonne à rien' and did not deserve to live. Brought face to face with Léa, she claimed not to recognize her ('elle est bien gentille mais ce n'est pas ma soeur',[27] Dupré 1984: 188). In May of that year she was moved to the public asylum in Rennes, where she died of a lung infection consequent upon

---

[26] 'A calm, measured town, where nobody gets worked up, even about a sensational trial . . . One must not judge the population as a whole on the basis of two madwomen, for we remain convinced that the two criminal sisters were not in full possession of their faculties.'
[27] 'she is very nice, but she's not my sister.'

self-inflicted malnutrition on 18 May 1937. Her clinical records were destroyed in the 1944 bombing of the city.

Léa was released, with two years' remission for good conduct, in 1943. Legally prohibited from residing in Le Mans, she went to the Loire estuary city of Nantes, some fifty miles away. Her mother had not visited her in prison, contenting herself with sending a few affectionate letters; yet it was with her that Léa was to live until Clémence's death, almost as though life on her own were unbearable, even incomprehensible, to her. Her name, for public consumption at any rate, was no longer 'Léa'; she opted instead to be known as 'Marie', the criminal label driven out by the supreme signifier of redemptive female innocence. She was tracked down in 1966 by a *France-Soir* journalist, whose article compares her to a '[s]pectre du passé qui brûle au point de la réduire à la couleur de la cendre'[28] (Dupré 1984: 201). She worked as a chambermaid and cleaning-woman, living a life of tranquil anonymity in the same kind of minute but tidy room that she must have occupied in the rue Bruyère, and keeping mementoes of Christine and lace from the Lancelin house among her possessions. She was widely believed to have died in 1982, but as the Afterword will show was still alive in 2000.

M. Lancelin, unable to sell his house after the dreadful event there, lived in 6 rue Bruyère with a housekeeper until his death some twenty years after the crime. The house has since changed hands at least twice. In the summer of 1999 at least, it was the only one in its street not to bear a number.

---

[28] 'a ghost of the past that has burnt her until she is the colour of ash.'

2 Mirrors, Fusions, and Splittings

The Papins, the *fait divers*, and the Psychoanalysts

Why the *fait divers*?

Interest in the *fait divers*—for which the only approximation to an English-language equivalent seems to be the somewhat feeble 'human interest story'—has increased apace with the advent and growth of cultural studies, but the repercussions of the Papin case show that it goes back a good way beyond that. The first appearance of the term can be traced to *Le Petit Journal* in 1863, which links its emergence to that of the age of mass literacy. Christine and Léa seem to have had very little interest in reading (though Christine is said to have copied out poetry in her youth), but it is a fairly safe bet that many of the written texts that might have come their way would have been of the order of the *fait divers*, requiring none of the cultural background necessary for the reading of 'serious' news stories. For David Walker, the lack of an English translation for the term points to its 'specific function within French culture' (Walker 1995: 3)—due in part, we would surmise, to the acute polarity within France between 'sophisticated' metropolitan centre and 'backward' provincial periphery. Stendhal's *Le Rouge et le noir*, Hugo's *Les Misérables*, Foucault's *Surveiller et punir* and *Moi, Pierre Rivière* (the latter analysing a first-hand account of a bloody family slaying) are all examples of French high cultural texts that draw upon the *fait divers* or *fait divers*-like material. *Le Rouge et le noir* and *Les Misérables* are set amid times of intense social and political change, while *Surveiller et punir* begins with a famously grisly account of the execution of a would-be regicide. The Papin killings occurred at a time of growing political unrest in France, which was to issue in the right-wing riots of the following year and the period of disruption leading up to the short-lived Popular Front government. These years were also marked by the burgeoning of *fait divers* magazines—*Détective*, initially under the editorship of Joseph Kessel, was founded in 1928, to be followed by such as *Police Magazine* and, appropriately enough, *Fait divers*. All of this would seem to support Walker's definition of the *fait divers* as 'the form . . . that articulates political, historical and cultural information in terms which accord with our fantasms on involvement in the dramas of reality' (Walker 1995: 6).

The *fait divers*, in other words, is the point at which the private or trivial world gains sudden, arbitrary-seeming access to the public one. British and American public life have become increasingly permeable to gossip and scandal in the private sphere, as the Clinton presidency demonstrates, whereas the rigorous constitutional protection afforded to private life in France has ensured a much clearer separation of the two domains, so that the existence of Mitterrand's second family became public knowledge only with his consent. This may be another reason for the particular importance of the *fait divers* in French culture. Its very triviality is part of the reason for its omnipresence; it travels light, with only such cultural baggage as its reproducers and redeployers choose to give it, so that the use made of the Papin case by Genet or Beauvoir will be very different from that of readers fascinated by the sensational aspects of the sisters' crime. Very different from, but not wholly other than, for without such fascination the *fait divers* would never make the transition from ephemeral to high culture. A shamefaced *jouissance* is surely fundamental to interest in it, for to quote Merleau-Ponty 'Le goût du fait divers, c'est le désir de voir'[1] (Merleau-Ponty 1960: 388).

The *fait divers* has much in common with two other concepts widespread in recent French cultural theory—that of the *quotidien* or everyday and that of the 'event' in the sense in which the postmodern philosopher Jean-François Lyotard in particular uses the term. For Situationists such as Guy Debord and Raoul Vaneigem, influential in the politicization of everyday life that was to prove an important element in May 1968, and before them the dissident communist philosopher Henri Lefebvre, everyday life was not, or not only, a tissue of banalities to be brushed wearily aside; on the contrary, it called for especially close attention as the domain in which revolutionary social change was most likely to begin. For Lyotard the 'event' resides 'in the disruption . . . of a restricted narrative temporality' (Bennington 1988: 108); it is that which resists absorption into the tranquil automatism of the 'everyday' in its banally pejorative sense. The *Annales* school of history became prominent after the Second World War, was to be a major influence on Michel Foucault through its stress on what were previously considered minor cultural phenomena rather than on 'names and dates', and likewise has obvious affinities with the *fait divers*. In all these cases it is the combination of the routine and the extraordinary that is the common factor, bringing with it a sense that the *fait divers* (or

---

[1] 'Liking for the *fait divers* is rooted in the desire to see.'

the everyday, or the event) is rich with (a) sense(s) that cannot be entirely circumscribed.

This is what Georges Auclair is evoking when he refers to 'le mana quotidien'—'mana', a Polynesian term, is used to refer to the notion of Fate as some kind of determinate cause (Auclair 1970: 77). That fate need not strike with a single, unrepeatable blow, for one important observation made by Auclair is the existence of the 'fait divers à épisodes' (Auclair 1970: 62). Examples he gives include that of Violette Nozières, who was to die watched over by the mother she had attempted to kill, and the woman who inspired the villainess of Clouzot's 1943 film *Le Corbeau*, about poison-pen letters under the Occupation, who died peacefully in the provincial town of Tulle at the age of 81. This quality is doubly at work in the Papin case—in the chronicling of the participants' lives after the trial (Léa's life and reported death show clear similarities with those of the 'character' from *Le Corbeau*), and in the multiplicity of successive analyses, interpretations, and reproductions which have ensured—up to and including the present text—that new episodes to the story are always being written.

The notion of fate in its classical sense is of course imbued with mystical overtones that will be unacceptable to a majority of contemporary readers. Auclair assimilates it to a Freudian 'retour fantasmatique du refoulé' (Auclair 1970: 207), and earlier speaks of it as a 'projection globale de la symbolique du Père prise dans toute son ambiguïté'[2] (Auclair 1970: 83). We have already seen how the Papin case can be viewed as a return of the French provincial repressed, but its connection with the 'symbolique du Père' is perhaps less clear. The ultimate foreclosure in the case, after all, is that of the father—from the abandoned and disgraced Gustave through to the hapless M. Lancelin, standing bemused and an unknowing widower on the doorstep of his own house in a paradigmatic gesture of male exclusion. For Nicole Ward Jouve, 'the lack of a father figure of any kind is what made the situation ultimately murderous: in Kleinian terms, no penis on to which to project and redirect the aggression against the bad breast' (Ward Jouve 1998: 80).

If, however, we understand Auclair's formulation in relation less to the facts of the Papin case than to the various ways in which they have been told—as pertaining, that is to say, to their enunciations rather than their enunciated—it becomes much more accessible. The 'non/nom du Père'—the Father's name, but also his refusal of the male infant's sexual

---

[2] 'a fantasmatic return of the repressed . . . the overall projection of the symbolic of the Father grasped in all its ambiguity.'

desire for the mother—is for Lacan (whom nobody has ever accused of not being a phallocrat) the necessary condition for access to the symbolic order of language, and hence to any kind of narrative. Allusions at the trial and in the press to the sisters' lack of interest in 'young men' suggest that part of the bemusement the case provoked was connected with the absence of a symbolic Father-figure, as if aggression directed against M. Lancelin might have seemed more recuperable. The successive recountings and analyses of the story can in this context be seen as so many attempts to bring the killings back into the comparative safety of patriarchal narrative law, of which the *fait divers* is a homely but telling example.

Classical fate, for Auclair, equates with what he terms a 'surplus de signifiant' (Auclair 1970: 235)—a phrase that could describe the proliferation of texts on the Papin affair from 1933 to the present day. That surplus is at the same time never enough, for the more discourses are proffered on the affair the more inexhaustible it, and they, seem. The sisters' own inarticulacy appears like a virgin page on which the temptation to write is endless, and the mass of those writings go to make up what for Auclair is the essence of the *fait divers*.

The journalistic texts considered in the previous chapter obviously fall under the heading of the *fait divers*, providing us already with evidence that its concern is less 'la réalité statistique du crime que les fantasmes que la collectivité forme à son sujet'[3] (Auclair 1970: 123). This chapter will interrogate some of the most significant of those 'fantasmes', beginning with two particularly striking examples from the journalism of the time. The trial was covered for *Paris-Soir* by the Tharaud brothers, Jérôme and Jean, who invariably signed their stories in the first person singular ('de notre envoyé spécial, Jérôme et Jean Tharaud').[4] So bizarre a replication of the sibling fusion and identification that characterized the Papins clearly calls for further investigation, the more so as the brothers' reports are among the most perspicacious on the case. Janet Flanner, for forty-six years author of a fortnightly 'Letter from Paris' in the *New Yorker*, wrote a piece shortly after the trial remarkable for its wit and gender awareness. Onomastic serendipity—the fate of the *fait divers* in action?—dictated that she signed her columns 'Genêt'.

The affair might have been expected to arouse such horror and revulsion in Le Mans that all traces of it would have been meticulously buried. Such, however, is not the case. Paulette Houdyer's *L'Affaire Papin*, to be discussed in Chapter 3, was republished in 1988 by the Le Mans-based Cénomane after having been long out of print with its original publisher,

---

[3] (less) 'the statistical reality of the crime than the phantasms the community constructs around it.'

[4] 'by our special correspondent, Jérôme and Jean Tharaud.'

René Julliard, and two Le Mans magazines, *La Vie mancelle* and *Cénome*, were to publish articles on the case looking back from many years later, which will be of interest in our view of the affair as symptomatic of *la France profonde*.

The bulk of this chapter, however, will be given over to the major psychoanalytical and sociological treatments of the Papins—Lacan and Dupré, as already suggested, but also Louis Le Guillant's view of them as class warriors. Our aim here will not be to privilege one of those readings over the others nor indeed to pass judgement (other than adventitiously) on any of them. The Papin affair, like any *fait divers*, exists and is available only as a palimpsest, in and through the successive variety of reproductions of it—what Francis Dupré has called its 'on-dit'. To 'understand' it—as the quotation marks suggest *stricto sensu* an impossibility—can only mean to bring those reproductions together and see what light they shed, and what shadows they cast, on one another.

'La Règle du je': the strange case of the Tharaud brothers

The literary culture of France, like most others, contains its fair share of eccentric or otherwise mildly interesting minor writers—the breed for whom the term bellettrist, of seventeenth-century French origin, was coined. The interest of such figures is often a contextual rather than a more narrowly textual one, residing in what they represented rather than in what they actually wrote. Examples might include Xavier de Maistre at the turn from the eighteenth to the nineteenth century, at the end of the latter century that Comte Robert de Montesquiou who supposedly served as the model for Proust's Baron de Charlus, and nearer to our own day such members of the *Hussards* group as Antoine Blondin and Jean-Louis Curtis.

Even in what is by definition a comparatively esoteric group, Jérôme and Jean Tharaud occupy a minor place. Their work—characteristically for bellettrists—is an amalgam of novels, travel books, commentaries on current affairs, and other pieces of journalism. Their biographer Yvonne Foubert-Daudet comments that 'Le tragique fait divers semble, en effet, avoir hanté leur production littéraire'[5] (Foubert-Daudet 1982: 27), and as we have seen the brothers always signed that production in the first person singular—whence the title of Foubert-Daudet's book, *La Règle du*

---

[5] 'Their literary production seems to have been haunted by the tragic *fait divers*.'

je. Jérôme, who studied at the École Normale Supérieure, appears to have been the dominant partner (Jean, by contrast, failed his entrance examination for the Finance Ministry), but any discrepancy between the two brothers was occluded by their common signature—uncannily similar to that which the Papin sisters appended to their crime. Like the Goncourts of whom their lives in many ways resemble an echo (they won the eponymous prize in 1906), they remained bachelors for most of their lives, Jérôme marrying in 1916 at the age of 52 and Jean, the younger by three years, not until just before his death in 1952. His relationship with Hélène, whom he was to marry, led to a quarrel with his brother that was never patched up, and of which Foubert-Daudet says: 'Leur vraie mort demeure cependant ces dernières années où ils avaient vécu séparés, déchirés'[6] (Foubert-Daudet 1982: 181). Could these words not also have been said of Christine and Léa?

What is most striking about their reports on the trial for *Paris-Soir* is the absence of a condemnatory tone, and their awareness of how mysterious the case was. One of their dispatches is headlined: 'Jugées et condamnées, les soeurs Papin n'ont pas encore livré leur secret'[7] (Dupré 1984: 123). The brothers were for most of their careers situated on the political right, despite Jérôme's youthful flirtation with anarchism and *Dreyfusard* tendencies. He was later to work as secretary to the right-wing nationalist writer Maurice Barrès, and both brothers displayed marked anti-semitic tendencies and supported Mussolini's invasion of Ethiopia. Yet their writings on the Papins display a seemingly genuine curiosity to understand a sibling narcissism that cannot have failed, whether or not they acknowledged the fact, to remind them of their own. They write of the 'paper-scene', in which Léa is supposed to have been pinched until she bled to make her pick up a piece of paper, in terms that unmistakably evoke the unconscious: 'Mais le souvenir de cette scène n'était-il pas resté quelque part profondément en elle dans ces régions où s'agitent tant et tant de choses de nous-mêmes qui ne sont pas celles de la conscience claire?'[8] (*Littoral* 1983). Their texts are not without condescension, in their aesthetic dwelling on Léa's 'teint mat, olivâtre' or both sisters' 'fronts bien dessinés de personnes intelligentes, bien qu'elles ne le soient ni l'une ni l'autre'[9] (Dupré 1984: 86). Such

---

[6] 'Their real death, however, took place in those final years during which they had lived separately, torn apart.'

[7] 'Judged and condemned, the Papin sisters have not yet yielded up their secret.'

[8] 'But had the memory of this scene not remained deep within her, in those regions filled with so many agitated parts/objects of ourselves that do not belong to the realm of clear consciousness?'

[9] 'dull, olive complexion . . . finely chiselled foreheads of intelligent persons, though neither of them is such.'

condescension extends, at least implicitly, to the unfashionable city in which they had lived, for the sisters are described as primitive 'au sens qu'il [sc. that word] a quand on parle d'une société primitive'[10] (*Paris-Soir*, 30 Sept. 1934). There is a bewildered ethnographer's curiosity about the brothers' assertion that 'l'esprit du temps au milieu duquel elles vivent ne les a même pas effleurées'[11] (*Paris-Soir*, 30 Sept. 1934)—Paris almost scandalized by the depths of *la France profonde* and its igrorance. But it is noteworthy that the Tharauds' conclusion from the baffling distance between the trivial catalyst for the crime and its horrifying form is not that the Papin sisters were evil, but that they were almost undoubtedly mad:

> Mais entre un état irritable et le massacre qu'elle a fait, s'interpose l'image tragique, impénétrable, qui a pris devant moi sur la muraille la forme des deux soeurs et qui s'appelle: la folie.
>
> Je n'aurais rien su du procès, que rien qu'en les voyant (et je les verrai longtemps en esprit) aussi saisissantes l'une que l'autre dans leurs attitudes différentes, j'aurais eu immédiatement l'impression de me trouver devant l'anormal, l'inexplicable, l'inexpliqué.[12] (Dupré 1984: 87)

The Tharauds' attitude did not pass unchallenged. *Gringoire*, a satirical weekly politically associated with the far right, launched a strong attack on them, wholeheartedly endorsing the jury's verdict and declaring in terms worthy of a twenty-first-century tabloid: 'La société ne veut pas devenir un champ d'expériences cliniques où les victimes ne serviraient qu'à éclairer la psychologie des assassins'[13] (Dupré 1984: 122). Yet, through the degree of literary prestige they enjoyed at the time, their comments on it almost certainly had a significant effect. Their conclusion—'Un supplément d'enquête s'imposait'[14] (*Paris-Soir*, 1 Oct. 1934)—is substantially similar to that of Dr Logre. Nor is it very far removed from the 'guilty but insane' verdict implied by *Le Bonhomme sarthois*'s Gros-René—in his name and the bovine calm he ascribes to his city's inhabitants the very type of the 'société primitive' that so struck the Parisian

---

[10] 'in the sense the word has when applied to a primitive society.'

[11] 'the spirit of the times in which they live has not so much as touched them.'

[12] 'But between a state of irritation and the massacre that was its result there comes the tragic, impenetrable image which took on the wall in front of me the form of the two sisters and whose name is madness. Even had I known nothing of the case, merely on sight of them (and I shall see them in my mind for a long time), each as striking as the other in their different attitudes, I would at once have felt as if I were in the presence of the abnormal, the inexplicable, the unexplained.'

[13] 'Society has no desire to become a clinical experiment in which victims serve simply to illuminate the psychology of their murderers.'

[14] 'Further investigation was required.'

Tharauds. The popular press displayed in this case at least more acumen than the court of law.

From a distance: Janet Flanner and the 'anniversary' accounts

North Americans have long entertained an extremely close relationship with Paris, for reasons that are not far to seek. It is continental Europe's premier intellectual and cultural capital and the only one consistently to rival New York on the world stage, as well as having been in pre-jumbo jet days the most accessible from the United States. That special relationship has often been particularly intense where women—above all gay women—are concerned. 'The freedom and independence of foreign women in Paris during the twenties is well known' (Fitch 1985: 135–6). Gertrude Stein, Alice B. Toklas, Djuna Barnes, Sylvia Beach (owner of the Shakespeare and Co. bookshop in Paris which first published Joyce's *Ulysses*) were all important figures in the city's literary and cultural life in the 1920s and 1930s, and Janet Flanner, with her companion Solita Solano, formed part of the same set.[15]

Flanner/'Genêt''s piece on the Papin affair is remarkable in several respects. It treats the killing with an arch irony that would probably have been impossible for French journalists, culturally so much closer to the case. That irony instantly grasps the political implications of what is described as 'not a murder but a revolution', as well as the Gothic aesthetic of its 'paranoiac poetry and one of the most graceless murders in French annals' (Flanner 1972: 98)—the poetry that her neo-homonym was to render in *Les Bonnes*, the gracelessness that his reconstruction was to efface. The treatment of Mme Lancelin and Geneviève's bodies as foodstuffs, to be observed also by Dupré, is encapsulated in Flanner's account of how 'their modest limbs had been knife-notched the way a French baker notches his finer long loaves'. Is there a mnemic trace here of the two rolls ('petits pains') found at the scene of the crime? We have been unable to verify whether or not contemporary newspapers printed the girls' name as Lapin, rather than Papin, but were at first puzzled by the statement that this 'was no libel' (Flanner 1972: 99). Rabbits, after all, are resolutely herbivorous creatures and notorious for their fecundity, so

---

[15] Noel Riley Fitch's *Sylvia Beach and the Lost Generation* (Fitch 1985) and Greta Schiller's 1995 film *Paris was a Woman* provide illuminating coverage of this and other American intellectual groupings in Paris.

might well consider themselves doubly libelled by the misprint. Flanner's point becomes clearer when she postulates that the sisters were either 'normal girls who had murdered without a reason' or 'mad as March Hares'. She is unforgiving where the Tharauds—who wrote 'without logic and in unison' (Flanner 1972: 100)—are concerned, and little less so for the jury, 'twelve good men and true, or quite incompetent to appreciate the Papin sisters'. This is the only reference we have been able to find to the manifest absurdity of having a case that involved only women tried entirely by males (women were not entitled to sit on juries until they got the vote, at the Liberation).

The sisters' incestuous relationship is a trifle airily dismissed as 'one of the slighter details of their dubious domesticity' (Flanner 1972: 101), unlike Christine's hallucinatory and delirious behaviour, which Lacan is praised for being the first to take seriously. Flanner's reading of this is rich, sometimes excessively so, as when she asks apropos of Christine's 'Dis oui!' outburst: 'By what chance did this Sarthe peasant fall like the Irish Joyce in the last line of *Ulysses* on the two richest words in any tongue—those of human affirmation, *Yes, yes* . . . ?' (Flanner 1972: 102). Condescension and aestheticization, which we have seen are a besetting risk in dealing with this case, shadow the writing uneasily here, as in Flanner's conclusion that when Christine fell to her knees at the end 'At last she had heard the voice of God' (Flanner 1972: 104). What is interesting about Flanner's observations is the twofold otherness that stems from her being an American woman—the first member of either category, so far as we know, to have published comments on the case. The distinction between the Tharauds' seriousness, sometimes verging on the po-faced, and Flanner's sassy wit is clearly overdetermined by considerations of nationality and gender. *L'Humanité* too, as we have seen, paid, in its remarks on the case, an attention to gender largely atypical of the time, but its attitude towards the sisters' class origins is a far more unequivocally militant one. At the same time, it pays less heed than the sometimes supercilious-seeming Flanner to the sisters as individuals, treating them rather as metonymic representatives of their (gendered) class. Flanner's observation that 'In the chill pre-dawn both sisters' coat collars were turned up as if they had just come in from some domestic errand run in the rain' (Flanner 1972: 104) has in its attention to detail the ring of the realist novel. More than any other contemporary chronicler of the case she brings Christine and Léa alive as human beings. More even than that: in her claim that 'The Papins' was the pain of being two where some mysterious unity had been originally intended' (Flanner 1972: 103), she goes to the heart of the themes of sundering and mirroring so fundamental to the crime.

La mode rétro in an unexpected place: retrospectives on the affair

La mode rétro is an expression that generally evokes nostalgia for a bygone era of innocence—not so distant as all that in France because of the nation's belated industrialization, which took place in earnest only after the Second World War. The French cinema was awash with nostalgia films in the 1980s and (to a lesser extent) the 1990s, but it would be an oversimplification to see this as a uniformly idyllic phenomenon. The years between the death of President Georges Pompidou in 1974, which marked the effective end of a historic Gaullism grounded in the myth of universal Resistance, and that of ex-President François Mitterrand in 1996, after revelations about his ambiguous attitudes during *les années noires*, were a period of extended, and often agonized, historical scrutiny. (It would certainly be possible to view the vogue for nostalgia films as in part an attempt to offset this protracted culpabilization of the national past.) Novels such as Patrick Modiano's *La Place de l'Étoile*, or films such as Louis Malle's *Lacombe Lucien*, made the nation uncomfortable through their calling into question the foundations of what Benedict Anderson would call its 'imagined community'. On a less explicitly political level, the same can be said of Foucault's *fait divers*-based texts such as *Moi, Pierre Rivière*, whose evocation of sanguinary family tensions in *la France profonde* has already been mentioned.

Those tensions, like the destabilization of gender norms at work in the nostalgia film, are also figured in the Papin case and in its continual revisitings. It is thus less surprising than it may seem that three Le Mans publications revived the affair in the period between 1966 and 1984. Paulette Houdyer published 'Il y a trente-trois ans, les "filles" Papin'[16] in the September 1966 number of *La Vie mancelle*, to coincide with the first publication of her book *L'Affaire Papin*. Here she remembers hearing the news from a school friend who lived in the rue Bruyère, and speaks of the case as a moment 'Quand la province lave son linge sale en famille'[17] (Houdyer 1966). Houdyer's distinctive approach, in this article as in her book, is a regionalist one. She has spoken to us of her visceral loyalty to her province and of how she had worked on the case 'out of chauvinism', anxious to show that the social and emotional complexities of the Sarthe went far deeper than the department's numerous detractors might believe. To claim a spectacularly bloody killing for the credit of the

---

[16] 'Thirty-three years ago, the Papin "girls".'
[17] 'When the provinces wash their dirty linen in public.'

province in which it occurred is perhaps a slightly perverse undertaking, but not altogether an illogical one.

Dominique Robillon, in the spring 1981 number of *Cénome*, characterizes Houdyer's approach to the case as an 'étude des moeurs sarthoises'.[18] *L'Affaire Papin* is one of three reproductions of the case he briefly considers, along with *Les Bonnes* and Nico Papatakis's 1963 film *Les Abysses*. For Robillon, the killings were primarily the work of Christine, described as 'une psychopathe qui entraîne sa soeur dans sa folie meurtrière'.[19] S/he (we have been unable to gender the writer) opines that if the sisters' mental state was not taken into account at the trial this was because of reluctance to divulge their incestuous relationship ('il eut [*sic*] été "inconvenant" d'étaler en public de telles relations "contre nature" '[20]—Robillon 1981: 64). That task was to be left to Lacan, and shortly afterwards Janet Flanner.

Jacques Chaussumier, in the March 1984 number of *La Vie mancelle*, recalls his father telling the story on the morning after the crime. Chaussumier's piece is unconcerned with either the sisters' mental state or the subsequent reproductions of the affair, though he does mention a (planned?) filmic adaptation by Gilles Cousin to which we have been unable to trace any further reference. His focus is rather on the effects of the killings upon him. 'Toute la nuit mon imagination m'avait fait apparaître les deux victimes sans yeux sur lesquelles s'acharnaient les brunes filles aperçues le matin même, place des Jacobins.'[21] The case gave the boy nightmares, and caused him to avoid the rue Bruyère for a long time afterwards; we seem here closer to the suburban or rural world of American Gothic—say David Lynch's *Blue Velvet* (1986) or even Hitchcock's *Psycho* (1960), with its eyeless woman at the climax—than to *la France profonde*. The verdict and sentence appear to have done little to allay his anxieties ('ce n'est pas le jugement, ni cette condamnation qui me rassurèrent et me firent oublier ce crime odieux'[22]). Chaussumier's condemnatory tone is surely linked with his class position; his father, a tradesman, had commented that 'ces femmes sont de nos clients'[23] (Chaussumier 1984: 31), and the 'odiousness' of their crime for him must have had to do not only with its bloodiness, but with its breaching of the barrier between the bourgeoisie and their servant clientele.

---

[18] 'a study of Sarthe customs and mores.'
[19] 'a psychopath who dragged her sister along in her murderous insanity.'
[20] 'it would have been "unseemly" to go into such "unnatural" relations in public.'
[21] 'All night long my imagination brought before me the two eyeless victims of the two dark-haired girls I had seen that very morning, in the Place des Jacobins.'
[22] 'neither the judgement nor the sentence reassured me or led me to forget this odious crime.'
[23] 'those women are customers of ours.'

'Nostalgia' may appear a surprising description for texts dealing with so unidyllic an event. Yet, in their evocation of a Le Mans much less sprawling then than it is now, 'écrasée sous la masse énorme de sa cathédrale'[24] (Houdyer 1966: 4), and of a world in which everybody knew everybody else and—with one spectacular exception—their own place, they do seem to partake in some degree of the *mode rétro*, to be suffused with nostalgia for the tranquillity so brutally disrupted by the Papins' crime. The socio-political upheavals of the years immediately after the killings were to culminate in the Second World War, which precipitated France's transformation into a full-blown industrial society. Le Mans was to be massively affected by that transformation. The town the Papins and their contemporaries knew survives so to speak in quotation marks, in the conservation area that is *le vieux Mans* and its neighbouring streets. Part of the fascination of the case is the window it offers on to a world that is closer to that of Balzac's *Scènes de la vie de province* than to the modern city of today.

The Lacanian mirror

Jacques Lacan ranks among the most prominent and contentious French thinkers of the twentieth century. The rereading of Freud which formed the basis of his work for upwards of fifty years has been immensely influential in domains a long way from the psychoanalyst's couch, such as literary theory, gender studies, and film and media studies. There is not space here to do more than gesture towards some of that rereading's features most relevant to his paper on the Papin case. These include the centrality of language as constitutive of the human subject, and of gaps, silences, and more generally the unsaid as in their turn constitutive of that language; a foregrounding and privileging, influenced by Dali and the surrealists, of paranoia, seen as 'une activité créatrice logique'[25] (Roudinesco 1993: 56); and a stress on the importance of looking and of the gaze that underpins his concept of the 'stade du miroir' or mirror-phase, in which the child's recognition of its own image in a mirror paves the way for its access to the symbolic order of language. (Bowie (1991) is the best English-language introduction to this complex and controversial body of thought; Turkle (1979) helpfully situates it as a specifically French cultural phenomenon.)

---

[24] 'crushed beneath the great weight of the cathedral.'   [25] 'a logical creative activity.'

Christine and Léa's verbal inarticulacy broken by an occasional primitive eloquence ('Mon crime est assez grand pour que je dise ce qui est'),[26] their evident paranoia instanced well before the murder by their visit to the mayor, their destruction of the gazes that conferred upon them an identity they had come to resent mesh closely enough with Lacan's concerns for it to be clear why he was fascinated by their case. His paper on it was first published in the surrealist journal *Le Minotaure* in 1933. The surrealists were among the first in France to take Freud seriously, 'not least because he . . . regards the distinction between the normal and the abnormal as rather less than self-evident' (Macey 1988: 60), while the punning floridity and rejection of conventional linear logic so marked in Lacan's later work unmistakably bear the surrealist imprint.

The surrealists and Lacan had in common a far from innocent interest in the criminal or hysterical female, predating by many years Lacan's notorious observation on Bernini's statue of Saint Teresa ('elle jouit, ça ne fait pas de doute'[27]—Lacan 1975*a*: 97). Éluard and Péret wrote a short piece on the Papin sisters in the fifth issue of *Le Surréalisme au service de la révolution*, which will be discussed in Chapter 3, while Breton and Éluard were among contributors to a bizarre volume published in celebration of Violette Nozières. Lacan shared this somewhat suspect excitement, as his doctoral thesis, submitted and published in the year before the Papin killings, shows.

This text, *De la psychose paranoïaque dans ses rapports avec la personnalité*, reads curiously for those more familiar with the later Lacan, who agreed to its republication in 1975 only with reservations. The semantic pyrotechnics and barbed polemics of the later writings are absent; the paranoia is all in the written-about, not in the writing. The case he deals with is that of Marguerite Anzieu, née Pantaine, a post-office worker and part-time writer of romantic novels who in 1931 tried to stab to death the Parisian actress Huguette Duflos. Lacan's treatment of Mme Anzieu—'Aimée' as she is referred to throughout the thesis—was egotistical and imperialistic in the extreme, and he was obviously interested in her only as fodder for his reinscription of paranoia in a Freudian perspective. That reinscription bears striking resemblances to much that he was to say about the Papin case a couple of years later. Narcissistic fixation and homosexual drives are seen as constitutive elements of paranoia, itself viewed as a defence against desire. Thus, 'Le *persécuteur principal* est toujours *de même sexe* que le sujet, et est identique à, ou

---

[26] 'My crime is great enough for me to tell the truth.'
[27] 'she is coming, there is no doubt about it.'

tout au moins représente clairement, la personne du même sexe à laquelle le sujet tient le plus profondément par son histoire affective'[28] (Lacan 1975*a*: 273). This is true, for Lacan, of 'Aimée', who was reminded by Huguette Duflos of a woman she had been in love with many years before, and its relevance to the Papin sisters' relationship with their mother and Mme Lancelin scarcely needs pointing out. The central character of one of 'Aimée''s unpublished novels dreams of a sex change ('*Je vais être reçu garçon*, j'irai voir ma fiancée'[29]—Lacan 1975*a*: 185)—like Christine speaking of herself as her sister's husband—and a remark imputed to 'Aimée' by Lacan is premonitory of the tensions that must have built up between the Papins and the Lancelins ('Rien ne presse, se dit-elle, mais *là-bas l'orage s'amasse.*'[30]—Lacan 1975*a*: 164). Finally, it is worthy of note that Lacan stresses the intimate links between paranoia and self-punishment, evident in the sisters' refusal to seek any mitigation for their killing.

De la psychose paranoïaque thus functions as a clear pre-text for the piece on the Papins, *Motifs du crime paranoïaque: le crime des soeurs Papin*, as the presence of 'paranoïaque' in both titles may suggest. The later piece, stylistically modest though it still is, has more in common with the later, more familiar Lacan, notably in its foregrounding of the importance of speech and silence in the genesis of the crime:

> Servantes-modèles, a-t-on dit, enviées au ménage; servantes-mystère aussi, car, si l'on a remarqué que les maîtres semblent avoir étrangement manqué de sympathie humaine, rien ne nous permet de dire que l'indifférence hautaine des domestiques n'ait fait que répondre à cette attitude; d'un groupe à l'autre 'on ne se parlait pas'. *Ce silence pourtant ne pouvait être vide, même s'il était obscur aux yeux des acteurs* [italics added].[31] (Lacan 1975*a*: 389)

The electrical breakdown thus distilled and materialized the unspoken that lay at the heart of the sisters' relationship with each other and their employers, which is why it provoked such violence. Lacan gives an account of the killings and the trial largely drawn from the Tharauds' accounts, before going on to pay homage to Dr Logre's views on the case

---

[28] 'The *chief persecutor* is always *of the same sex* as the subject, and is identical to, or at least clearly represents, the person of the same sex to whom the subject is most deeply attached in his/her emotional history.'

[29] '*I am going to be accepted as a boy*, I shall go and see my beloved.'

[30] 'There's no hurry, she tells herself, but *over there the storm is gathering*.'

[31] 'They were model servants, we are told, the envy of other households—but also mystery servants, for if it has been noted that their masters seem to have been strangely lacking in human sympathy, there is nothing which authorizes us to say that the servants' lofty indifference was merely a response to that attitude. Between one group and the other "nobody talked". *Yet this silence could not be an empty one, even if it was obscure in the participants' eyes*' (italics added).

and to announce his intention of going beyond them. Élisabeth Roudinesco draws a parallel between the 'Aimée' case and that of the Papins
when she states:

> Si Aimée avait agressé la comédienne qui, selon Lacan, incarnait son idéal du
> moi, les servantes Papin avaient massacré les dames Lancelin pour un motif
> équivalent: le véritable mobile du crime n'était pas la haine de classe, mais la
> structure paranoïaque à travers laquelle le meurtrier frappait l'idéal du
> maître qu'il portait en lui.[32] (Roudinesco 1993: 96)

The paranoiac structure detected by Lacan and Roudinesco was of
course itself grounded in and overdetermined by class hatred, but the
psychoanalytic focus on what might be termed the form or the enunciation of the killings accounts more fully for their peculiar violence than a
symptomatic sociological explanation on its own could do. That enunciation—what Dupré was later to call 'le passage à l'acte'[33]—passed
through a dreadful literalness exemplified by the electrical breakdown
(the French phrase 'le courant ne passe pas' is used to denote a lack of
communication, roughly equivalent to the English 'I'm not getting
through'), and climaxing in the blinding. Here 'les métaphores les plus
usées de la haine: "Je lui arracherais les yeux," reçoivent leur exécution
littérale'[34] (Lacan 1975a: 393). The shocking literalization commented
upon by Lacan hints at the madness and delirium at work beneath the
surface of 'normal' language.

All this is to say that the sisters' crime was, like the Lacanian unconscious, structured like a language—that the very excess of their paranoid
delirium was saying something. Lacan indicates this when he contrasts
the two views of psychosis prevalent at the time, one seeing it as inher-
ent in individuals ('un vice congénital du caractère'[35]), the other as 'un
effort rationnel du sujet pour expliquer ces expériences'[36] (Lacan 1975a:
392). The first view was clearly that expressed by the court of law, the
second is implicit in the inability of the Tharauds and others simply to
acquiesce in its verdict. It is as if Lacan were taking it upon himself to
provide the additional inquiry, the 'supplément d'enquête', that the Tharauds felt was required.

---

[32] 'If Aimée had attacked the actress who, for Lacan, incarnated her ideal self, the Papins had massacred Mme and Mlle Lancelin for a similar reason. The real motive for the crime was not class
hatred, but the paranoiac structure through which the murderers struck down the ideal master
they carried within themselves.'

[33] 'acting-out.'

[34] 'The most worn-out metaphors of hatred ("I'd tear her eyes out") are put into literal practice.'

[35] 'a congenital vice of character.'

[36] 'The subject's rational effort to explain his/her experiences.'

Lacan goes on to analyse Christine's remarks and behaviour in prison, finding a classic manifestation of paranoid delirium in her assertion: 'Je crois bien que, dans une autre vie, je devais être le mari de ma soeur.'[37] More than any previous text his is able to assimilate the killings to a framework (albeit a rapidly changing one) of comprehensibility, that of delirium *à deux* rooted in sado-masochism and homosexuality. The question he asks is self-evidently a rhetorical one: 'quelle signification ne prennent pas . . . l'affection exclusive des deux soeurs, le mystère de leur vie, les étrangetés de leur cohabitation, leur rapprochement peureux dans un même lit après le crime?'[38] (Lacan 1975*a*: 395). If he stops short of proclaiming the existence of an explicitly incestuous relationship, this would seem to be less out of prudishness than because it might have undercut his fundamental thesis, already expounded by Freud, that paranoia is a defence against same-sex desire. 'Cette tendance homosexuelle ne s'exprimerait que par une négation éperdue d'elle-même, qui fonderait la conviction d'être aimé et désignerait l'être aimé dans le persécuteur'[39] (Lacan 1975*a*: 395–6).

What is missing from Lacan's piece is a consideration of Christine and Léa's relationship with their mother, and of the partial transference of their feelings for her on to Mme Lancelin (of whom they sometimes spoke as 'maman'). Clémence's transformation from 'être aimé' to 'persécuteur' made of her the missing third (or fifth) party in the paranoid relationship. Léa's reconciliation with her on her release from prison appears in this light as a means of atonement (etymologically, 'at-one-ment') for the crime—reversing the transformation from persecutrix to loved one and thus retroactively undoing the paranoia that had erupted in the killings.

That at-one-ment could, however, come about only after Léa's sundering from Christine, which might appear to have taken place when the elder sister died or even when they were separated in prison, but which Lacan, in his first adumbration of the mirror-phase, situates much earlier—at the time, indeed in the very act, of the crime. 'Le stade du miroir permet d'insister sur l'amour que chacun d'entre nous porte à son image, sur la passion, qu'il entretient avec son moi chéri'[40] (Saint-Drôme

---

[37] 'I really believe that in another life I must have been/was meant to be my sister's husband.' (The French 'devais' refers ambiguously to a possible previous or parallel existence.)

[38] 'what might be the significance . . . of the two sisters' exclusive mutual affection, their mysterious life, their bizarre cohabitation, their fearful huddling together in one bed after the crime?'

[39] 'This [sc. paranoid] homosexual tendency is expressed only through a desperate denial of itself, which gives the conviction that one is persecuted and designates the beloved one as the persecutor.'

[40] 'The mirror-phase makes it possible to stress the love each one of us has for her or his image, the passion we entertain for our beloved self/ego.'

1994: 115). 'Aimée', already, had struck against a mirror-image of herself—'l'idéal qu'elle a de soi'[41] (Lacan 1975*a*: 397)—and the Papins were to do the same. Curiously, Lacan says next to nothing about Mme Lancelin ('Maman') or Geneviève, who was of a similar age to Christine. His concern is less with who or what the victims represented for Christine and Léa than with what they represented for each other, and the role the killings played in the resolution of their devouring reciprocal narcissism. '[I]l semble qu'entre elles les soeurs ne pouvaient même prendre la distance qu'il faut pour se meurtrir. Vraies âmes siamoises, elles forment un monde à jamais clos'[42] (Lacan 1975*a*: 397). The infant and its mirror-image, of course, can also be described as 'Siamese souls', and Lacan views the killing as a brutal operation (in both senses) of severance. His choice of vocabulary seems anything but innocent. Why 'meurtrir'—to bruise—rather than the more obvious 'blesser' (to hurt) or even 'se séparer'? The answer, surely, lies in the similarity of sound between 'meurtrir' and the noun 'meurtre' (murder). The play of the signifier is here suggesting that the sisters killed not (only) their exploiters or their mother, but each other, in a dementedly logical shattering of the mirror in which each could find and recognize herself only as the Siamese twin of the other.

Christine becomes, in the final paragraphs of Lacan's piece, something very like a tragic heroine—a peasant Electra in a world from which men were all but entirely absent, though we shall see in a moment that Lacan is able to find them at least an implicit place:

> **Quel long chemin de torture elle a dû parcourir avant que l'expérience désespérée du crime la déchire de son autre soi-même, et qu'elle puisse, après sa première crise de délire hallucinatoire, où elle croit voir sa soeur morte, morte sans doute de ce coup, crier devant le juge qui les confronte, les mots de la passion dessillée: 'Oui, dis oui.'[43]**

Again, the choice of vocabulary merits comment. 'Dessiller' in French originally meant to unstitch the eyes of a young falcon, which were sewn up to prevent it from taking premature flight. Christine's passion is thus literally 'unblinded', enabling her to see—literally and figuratively—Léa

---

[41] 'her ideal of herself.'

[42] 'It seems that the sisters could not even distance themselves sufficiently from each other to bruise each other. Real Siamese souls, they form a world forever closed in on itself.'

[43] 'What a long and tortured journey she must have had before the desperate experience of the crime tore her apart from her alter ego, before her first crisis of hallucinatory delirium when she thought she saw her sister dead—dead no doubt from the blow she had struck. Only then could she shout out, in the presence of the judge who brought them face to face, those words of a passion whose eyes were finally opened to itself: "Yes, say yes".'

as other than herself, in a 'normal' mirror bought of course at the terrible price of two all too real blindings.

Freud's distinctive contribution to the Oedipus myth—that part of it thenceforth known as the 'Oedipus complex'—was to read Oedipus's self-blinding as an act of self-castration, atonement for, and would-be retroactive destruction of, sexual desire for his/the mother. The Papin sisters—exemplars of an incest from which the male was excluded—are all but Oedipalized in Lacan's final paragraph, in which 'Elles arrachent les yeux comme châtraient les Bacchantes.'[44] The sexual nature of the mutilations to which Mme Lancelin and Geneviève were subjected is clear enough, the implication that that was a form of disavowal of Christine and Léa's desire for each other considerably less so. It is the choice of words and sounds, however, that is most fascinating. 'Arrachent', 'châtraient', 'Bacchantes' stand in a close phonetic relationship to one another, neither rhymes nor anagrams but partaking in some measure of both, as if to figure the deadly replication that was to issue in the murders. The previous sentence has done something similar ('C'est leur détresse qu'elles détestent dans le couple qu'elles entraînent dans un atroce quadrille'[45]—Lacan 1975*a*: 398), where the 'détresse/détestent' echo, the sing-song rhythm, the move from 'couple' to 'quadrille' seem to enact the lethal mirroring that is a leitmotif of the paper. Even at this early stage in his career, Lacan produced a piece whose interest lies as much in its choice and ordering of signifiers, its textual strategy, as in the substantive conclusions it draws.

Lacan mirrored: Francis Dupré's *passage à l'acte*

Dupré's La *'Solution' du passage à l'acte: le double crime des soeurs Papin* is considered here because it constitutes a development of, and commentary upon, *Motifs du crime paranoïaque*. It is also, as earlier chapters have suggested, an invaluable source of original French-language documentation on the case.

Dupré begins by contrasting two poles at one or other of which manifestations of madness are generally to be found:

> **D'un côté un discours parfois bavard, d'autres fois précautionneux, mais qui manque rarement de s'emparer de l'écrit pour son faire-savoir; c'est—exemplairement—Schreber. A l'autre pôle, la parole se trouve réduite à presque**

---

[44] 'They tear out eyes as the Bacchae used to castrate.'
[45] 'It is their own distress they detest in the couple they draw into an atrocious quadrille.'

rien, se présente comme résolument conventionnelle, et la folie paraît tout entière concentrée dans la seule effectuation du passage à l'acte. Ce sera— exemplairement—le cas dit des soeurs Papin.[46]

How To Do Things With Words is the title of a work by the linguistic philosopher J. L. Austin that has been immensely influential in France, where it is translated as *Quand dire, c'est faire/When speaking is doing*. The Papins' killings could easily be seen as a mirror-image of that title— *How to Say Things with Deeds* or *Quand faire, c'est dire*. Intellectual nature abhorring a verbal vacuum, it is unsurprising that the case has attracted so much textual attention—the *on-dit* (near-homophone of the *non-dit* or 'unsaid') to which Dupré makes frequent reference. Among the array of *on-dits* to which the case has given rise, pride of place goes to that of Lacan, for whom 'Le Moi du miroir est l'*on-dit* des soeurs Papin dans le frayage de la psychanalyse'[47] (Dupré 1984: 11).

The mirror-phase is important as the point at which sight and language, the visual and the verbal, meet. Thus it is that Dupré reproduces the 'before' and 'after' photographs of the sisters, for 'ce passage à l'acte fait transiter son dire par cette chicane d'une vision'[48] (Dupré 1984: 18), along with police photographs of the mutilated bodies—all forming part of the case's *on-dit*. The first half of his book is an exhaustive dossier on the trial and the reactions it provoked. It is in the fourth chapter ('Généalogie et chronologie') that Dupré's most original contribution makes itself felt, in his analysis of the sisters' relationship with their mother. Paulette Houdyer had already provided a graphic 'factional' account of this in *L'Affaire Papin*, but it was left to Dupré to provide on the one hand contemporary documentation (letters written by the sisters and Clémence), on the other close analysis of this fraught triangular relationship.

Clémence Derée testified after the killings that she had not spoken to her daughters since 1929, and that even when she ran into them in town they never answered her greeting—another silence to add to those already evoked by Lacan. She dated their final conversation to the second Sunday of October 1929, when she had gone to meet them and

---

[46] 'At one pole we find a sometimes verbose, sometimes prudent discourse which almost always makes itself known in writing; the archetypal example of this is Schreber. At the other, language is reduced almost to nothing, appearing resolutely conventional, and madness is concentrated entirely in the process of acting out. The archetypal example of this is the so-called Papin case.' The Schreber reference is to the celebrated, and verbally profuse, case of paranoia Freud analyses in *Psychological Notes on an Autobiographical Account of a case of Paranoia (Dementia Paranoides)*—the text in which the link between paranoia and same-sex desire is first articulated.

[47] 'The self/ego of/in the mirror is the *on-dit* of the Papin sisters in the path of psychoanalysis.'

[48] 'this acting-out says what it has to say by deflecting it through what it gives us to see.'

found them 'toutes changées à mon égard'[49] (Dupré 1984: 134). They had told her that earlier that day they had seen a lady who looked like her—unidentified, and for good reason, by Clémence—and had then bade her farewell and walked away, for what turned out to be the last time.

The disconcerting calmness of this episode, as relayed by Clémence, puts us once more in mind of the Freudian 'uncanny', the more so as for Freud themes of uncanniness 'are all concerned with the phenomenon of the "double" ' (Freud 1985: 356). To the doubling—from that day on narcissistically self-sufficient—of the two sisters corresponds that of their mother and the woman who looked like her. That woman, for Dupré, was none other than Mme Lancelin. With no access to relevant photographs of Clémence or Mme Lancelin, we have no way of knowing whether there was any physical resemblance; but even had there been one the sisters chose a most bizarre way of articulating it. What could be the sense of their enunciation?

Christine said that it was Mme Lancelin who had asked Clémence to give her and Léa more control over what they earned, as a result of which she was able to open a savings account—a benevolent intervention which Dupré brackets with Paulette Houdyer's assertion that the sisters spoke of their employer as 'maman' between themselves. This suggests to him a 'transfert maternel'[50] (Dupré 1984: 143)—what in Kleinian terms might be called a replacement of the original maternal bad breast by a potentially good one. This is plausible enough, but may leave us wondering why so seemingly positive a move as the rupture with an exploitative and uncaring mother should have had such hideous consequences.

Christine was widely said to be intolerant of any 'observation' made about her. (This translates most idiomatically as 'comment', but such a rendering loses sight of the visual connotations of 'observation'.) This was true alike of her mother and of her successive employers, leading Dupré to the conclusion that it must have been an unfavourable 'observation' from Mme Lancelin that led to the transference on to her of the sisters' feelings towards their mother. The factual evidence here, perhaps inevitably, is less than robust, but Dupré's hypothesis does suggest an explanation for the perceived resemblance between Mme Lancelin and Clémence—a *délire d'interprétation* based on behaviour rather than appearance, 'sur l'appui d'un trait'[51] as Dupré has it. The unnerving smoothness of the break with the real mother would then be accounted for by the (unconscious) fluency with which the sisters were able to promote Mme Lancelin to her place. Yet that place, we have seen, was

---

[49] 'quite changed where I was concerned.'   [50] 'maternal transference.'
[51] 'on the basis of an action.'

an emotionally charged one, from which the sisters had long been accustomed to being 'observed' in a manner Christine in particular had come to find intolerable. Dupré has earlier pointed out that the 'before' photograph of the sisters was taken for their mother, for whom it was obviously important that they should appear immaculately turned out. Mme Lancelin's observations to Christine about occasional lapses in cleaning were thus destined to stoke the fires of resentment against that Clémence whose place she had come to occupy. Furthermore, for Dupré, Christine was to become for Léa what Mme Lancelin became for Christine—'une mère aimante'.[52] The incestuous spiral between the sisters could only be intensified. '[L]a tension, dans la maisonnée Lancelin, monte d'un cran'[53] (Dupré 1984: 143).

The town hall episode and that involving the dropped piece of paper are adduced in support of this, Mme Lancelin's pinching of Léa seen as evidence that 'il est en son pouvoir de disposer de son corps, en laissant, de plus, une trace sur ce corps'[54] (Dupré 1984: 155). Dupré carries on where first Logre, then Lacan left off in treating Christine and Léa as a psychological couple ('âmes siamoises'), while stressing that Lacan's own text suggests the undoing of that couple through its concentration on Christine at the end. The couple, indeed, was never a symmetrical one. Léa's 'Pour moi, je suis sourde et muette' already indicates that by its subsumption of her words into her sister's, so that their relationship comes to resemble 'le redoublement du tissu et de sa doublure, de l'original et de sa copie, de la voix et de son écho'[55] (Dupré 1984: 165).

That 'redoublement' was not to survive; it came to an end with Christine's crisis on 12 July ('Dis-moi oui!'), which led to a '*méconnaissance systématique* de Léa'[56] (Dupré 1984: 167) that was never to change. This corroborates Lacan's view that the killings had served to detach the sisters from each other, for though Christine was to ask in a letter one week later for permission to see Léa she was never again to do so. The mirror was finally broken, Christine's earlier hallucinations that Léa was dead turning out in a sense at least to foreshadow the truth.

It was, of course, Christine who was to die first, of exhaustion brought on by her prolonged refusal to take nourishment. The sententious verdict of *Ouest-Éclair* ('Christine Papin a exécuté contre elle-même la peine de mort prononcée par la justice des hommes'[57]—Dupré 1984: 193) has

---

[52] 'a loving mother.'   [53] 'The tension in the Lancelin household rises.'

[54] 'that body was hers to dispose of, even to leave a mark on.'

[55] 'the reduplication of the cloth and its lining, the original and its copy, the voice and its echo.'

[56] 'a systematic misrecognition of Léa.'

[57] 'Christine Papin carried out on herself the death sentence passed on her by human judgment.'

more than a grain of truth about it, as her earlier refusal to sign an appeal against the death penalty shows. The 'passage à l'acte' marked by the killings could only be undone by a refusal to take action whose logical conclusion was death.

In his conclusion Dupré stresses much more than Lacan the asymmetrical relationship between the two sisters, complicated in any event by the existence of a third (Emilia) whom they never used to see. (We have not been able to establish what Emilia's response to the killings was, nor indeed any details of her life after her admission to the convent.) That asymmetry found an issue in the maternal transference on to Mme Lancelin, which was to flare into violence when Geneviève took her mother's part in the fatal dispute. '*Voir une fille prendre le parti de sa mère*, toute sa [sc. Christine's] vie n'avait de sens qu'à faire barrage à cette vision-là'[58] (Dupré 1984: 263). Once that sight, that vision, was before her, it had at all costs to be destroyed.

And so indeed it was. Christine escaped the Siamese mirror in which she was confined with Léa by shattering it, at the same time eliminating even the reflected possibility that Léa might return to her real mother. This, of course, she was to do, but only when Christine was no longer there. Lacan famously states, in his seminar on Edgar Allan Poe's *The Purloined Letter*, that 'une lettre arrive toujours à destination'.[59] That destination will not, however, be a simple or unequivocal one, for 'l'émetteur . . . reçoit du récepteur son propre message sous une forme inversée'[60] (Lacan 1966: 53)—the very process we have seen at work between Christine and Léa.

Whatever the claims to truth (or even Truth) of Lacan's *œuvre*—an infamously vexed question into which it is impossible to go here—it seems clear that for an understanding of the Papin sisters it, and its prolongation in Dupré's book, *work*, much as the deadly *passage à l'acte* worked for Christine and Léa (it was somewhat less successful for Mme Lancelin and Geneviève). Certain of Dupré's hypotheses and interpretations seem to us excessive and implausible, and these we have not gone into here. But his mirroring and development of Lacan's arguments indicate the dizzying complexities—of reflection, refraction, bondedness, and sundering—that were for so long at work between the Papins and

---

[58] '*A girl taking her mother's part*—the whole of Christine's life was meaningful only in so far as it blocked out that sight.'

[59] 'a letter always reaches its destination.' 'Lettre' ('l'être') here is to be understood as any act of linguistic communication, which for Lacan always involves the unconscious and thus can never be innocent or straightforward.

[60] 'the sender . . . receives from the receiver his own message in inverted form.'

those around them. In their *passage à l'acte*, the sisters said something—a great many things—that they could not conceivably have understood. Lacan and Dupré, for all our divergences from them, help us to understand.

Mothers and daughters: the reading of Marie-Magdeleine Lessana

The mother–daughter relationship has latterly begun to emerge from the shadow into which Freud's prioritizing of the Oedipus complex had banished it. Marie Cardinal and Julia Kristeva are two of the best-known names associated with its reinscription, in very different types of psychoanalytic perspective. To their names can now be added that of Marie-Magdeleine Lessana, who in *Entre mère et fille: un ravage* scrutinizes mother–daughter relationships across texts as different as the *Lettres* of Mme de Sévigné, the life of Marlene Dietrich, Marguerite Duras's *Le Ravissement de Lol V. Stein*, and the case of Marguerite Anzieu—Lacan's 'Aimée'. The concept of 'ravage' is used by Lessana to denote the unavowed hatred present in the mother–daughter relationship and the trauma inflicted upon the daughter by this. That hatred has its roots in the fact that 'mère et fille expérimentent réellement le "devenir femme" de la fille'[61] (Lessana 2000: 397). The mimetic eroticism this engenders is one with no possible resolution within the relationship, so that it is perceived as 'obscene' and arouses persecutory violence, clearly present in all the case-studies of which the book is made up. 'Si la particularité du féminin n'est pas identificatrice, mais l'expérience d'une désertion de l'obscénité maternelle, à côté et au-delà du rapport au phallus, en vérité les femmes ne sauraient faire communauté des femmes, comme femmes'[62] (Lessana 2000: 403).

This is a gloomy-seeming prognosis, attenuated by the satisfactory resolution of the 'ravage' in the case of Mme de Sévigné in particular, and by the text's concluding call—reminiscent of what Anglo-Americans call queer theory—to 'soutenir une sexuation qui ne réponde plus à l'ambition d'être femme, ni à celle d'être différente de l'homme, elle subvertit

---

[61] 'mother and daughter really live through the daughter's "becoming a woman".'
[62] 'If the specificity of the feminine is not identificatory, but the experience of desertion of/by maternal obscenity, at once alongside and beyond the relationship to the phallus, then the truth is that women can never form a community as women.'

la différence'[63] (Lessana 2000: 404). Christine and Léa's relationship might well have been their way of achieving this, but it is difficult to tell since one very disconcerting feature of Lessana's text is that she makes no overt reference to its sexual dimension. Drawing largely on Dupré, she emphasizes the 'caractère de pureté'[64] (Lessana 2000: 346) of the crime and the fact that it was 'porteur d'un savoir insu'[65] (Lessana 2000: 347). Her focus is almost entirely on Christine; indeed her chapter bears the title 'Christine Papin, ou l'émancipation impossible', foreclosing the subservient Léa and all but absolving her of responsibility for the crime fully assumed by the elder sister alone.

Lessana is the only writer on the case to dwell on the fact that Geneviève, Christine, and Léa were all menstruating at the same time. The malfunctioning iron thus meant that '[l]es pantalons (culottes) tachés de sang de Mademoiselle étaient peut-être mêlés à ceux de Christine et Léa'[66] (Lessana 2000: 350), in the uncomfortable cross-class proximity of the laundry basket—an analogy perhaps for the confused and bloody ballet of identifications that was about to take place? Most significant of these for Lessana is that between Christine and Geneviève— 'la seule avec qui Christine ait voulu répliquer au coup par coup, en miroir dans l'agression'[67] (Lessana 2000: 358). The mirror here evoked, as for Dupré, reflected back to the sisters their own couple in the form of Mme Lancelin and Geneviève, 'dans la fulgurance'[68] (Lessana 2000: 359)—an expression on which it is worth dwelling. Lightning, even—or especially—reflected in a mirror, can be so bright that it dazzles, precluding clear perception of that which it illuminates. Christine (and to a far lesser extent Léa) 'saw', but did not see what it was she saw, and that simultaneity of what Paul de Man has called *Blindness and Insight* (de Man 1983) was to find its resolution in the 'passage à l'acte' that was the blinding of the two Lancelin women.

Two mirrored sets of Siamese twins, then—a structure figured in the 'before and after' photographs, and familiar from the other readings of the case we have examined. What Lassena, not untendentiously, adds to these is the 'impossibilité échue à Christine: celle de devenir mère d'une fille'[69] (Lessana 2000: 360). The daughter's status as potential mother in

[63] 'to sustain a process of sexuality which no longer fulfils the ambition to be a woman nor to be different to a man, but rather subverts difference.'

[64] (The killings') 'quality of purity.'   [65] 'it was the bearer of an unknown knowledge.'

[66] 'Mademoiselle's bloodstained knickers (or pants) were perhaps mixed in with Christine's and Léa's.'

[67] 'the only one to whom Christine responded blow by blow, in a mirror of aggression.'

[68] 'in a flash of lightning.'

[69] 'the impossibility for Christine to become the mother of a daughter.'

her turn lies for her at the heart of the 'ravage', even more markedly perhaps for Christine who 'ne connut pratiquement aucun ravage direct avec sa mère'[70] (Lessana 2000: 396) than for the other daughters she scrutinizes. The maternal transference on to Mme Lancelin, and through her on to her daughter who might (have) become the mother Christine would never be, is clearly at work here. 'Cet instant de rencontre pure, réelle, a fait exploser les termes même de cette impossibilité'[71] (Lessana 2000: 360).

This might have been more convincing had Lessana stated more clearly the reasons for the 'impossibility' to which she refers. She speaks of the extreme closeness of the sisters as compensating for Christine's inability to bear a daughter of her own, and hints at an explanation for this in her account of Clémence's at once distant and possessive behaviour, the sign of 'un amour tyrannique et totalitaire, parasité par son revers de haine adressée aux éventuels rapteurs de ses filles'[72] (Lessana 2000: 364). What remains unsaid, in a perspective which despite the conclusion's genuflection to queer theory certainly smacks of the heteronormative, is the sexual quality of the sisters' relationship. That, as we have seen, made each of them all at once mother, daughter, and 'wife-husband'—remember Christine's fantasy about their previous conjugal life—to the other—a solipsistic bond which kept Clémence (to say nothing of unwelcome suitors) at bay, but at the cost of transferring the 'ravage' on to the Lancelin women.

Lessana identifies a key moment in this transference as that when Mme Lancelin began paying the sisters their wages directly, in 1929, which provoked what was to be for Christine at least the final breach. 'Le lien de service entre les bonnes et leurs patrons s'est reserré, les filles sont passées sous la coupe de Mme Lancelin'[73] (Lessana 2000: 370). The irony here is disquieting; the emancipatory gesture of an enlightened employer was to be her death sentence. The two surviving letters written by Clémence to her daughters in 1931 are analysed in sufficient detail to reveal them as despairing, but unavailing, attempts to regain maternal control (to work through the 'ravage'?). It was two years too late. The lethal transference had already occurred.

The final paragraph of Lessana's chapter follows the uncontentious assertion that 'Christine en son acte fait le ravage avec Mme Lancelin'

---

[70] (Christine) 'experienced virtually no direct ravaging with her mother.'

[71] 'This moment of pure, real encounter blew apart the very terms of that impossibility.'

[72] 'a tyrannical and totalitarian love, parasitized by its obverse of hatred directed at the possible abducters of her daughters.'

[73] 'The bond between the maids and their employers became tighter, and the girls fell under Madame Lancelin's power.'

with a speculation that Christine's statement that 'Elle [Mme Lancelin] lança ses deux bras dans ma direction'[74] was a play on or trace of the name 'Lancelin'. That Mme Lancelin's gesture was at once aggressive and possessive, a pushing away and a pulling towards, there can be little doubt, but that would have been the case even had she been called 'Dupont'. Here as in the fantasy (but whose fantasy?) of the bloody laundry-basket, a taint of *délire d'interprétation* may be suspected. Notwithstanding this and her implicit heteronormativeness, Lessana's reading complements and extends Lacan's and Dupré's in a number of important ways. It inserts the killings into a newly important psychoanalytical and theoretical perspective; it sheds new light on the importance of the transference from Clémence on to Mme Lancelin; and in so doing it makes the killings seem more clearly Christine's doing than in any other account, giving them an air of inevitability. If Christine realized her 'ravage', its literally tragic victim was Mme Lancelin.

The killings as class revenge: Louis Le Guillant's reading

In 1963, when the psychiatrist Louis Le Guillant published 'L'Affaire des soeurs Papin' in *Les Temps modernes*, that journal, founded by Sartre and Merleau-Ponty in 1944, was almost certainly the most influential intellectual publication in France. The mid and late 1960s were to see the rise of *Tel Quel*, emblematic of the supplanting of existentialism by structuralism as the dominant tendency in Parisian intellectual life. Le Guillant's article appeared three years before the publication of Foucault's *Les Mots et les choses* and Lacan's *Écrits* (though the texts that make up the latter had for the most part already been published separately), which consecrated that supplanting.

The intellectual and political tradition in which *Les Temps modernes* situated itself was that of *engagement* or commitment, most comprehensively espoused in the life and work of its co-founder Sartre. This extended on to the plane of social action the Sartrean view that human beings existed and were constituted only in and through their relations with others. The ethical code (for that is what it was) of *littérature engagée* 'called for the writer to disclose and correct the full range and variety of injustice he or she encountered' (Ungar 1998: 482), which in the bipolar context successively of Occupation,

---

[74] 'Christine in her act worked through her ravagement with Mme Lancelin . . . "She flung both her arms towards me".'

Resistance, and the Cold War generally equated with a strong political commitment to the Left.

Les Temps modernes thus combined philosophical analysis and dissection with work of a much more polemical and journalistic nature, and Le Guillant's article provides an excellent example of this. He encountered Lacan's piece as the article was about to go to press, so that it is referred to only in a footnote, where praise for 'la qualité et la richesse de son analyse' is slightly mitigated by the fact that 'elle ne comporte aucune allusion au fait que Christine et Léa étaient des domestiques'[75] (Le Guillant 1963: 907). It is the issue of social class, as in *L'Humanité*'s coverage at the time of the trial, that is paramount for Le Guillant, whose piece thus complements Lacan's rather than conflicting with it. The attitude towards psychoanalysis in Sartrean circles at the time was an ambivalent one; early hostility (doubtless influenced by the Communist Party) had been replaced by a more nuanced critical fascination, and Sartre had written the screenplay for John Huston's 1962 biopic *Freud: The Secret Passion*. His theories of subjectivity and freedom, however, were in sharp contrast with those of Lacan, whom he was to denounce as complicit with the bourgeoisie.[76] Le Guillant's epigraph, already quoted ('*Moi pas chien, moi humain*'), serves notice that his treatment of the case will be a strongly committed one, issuing in the claim that 'la condition des domestiques constitue la persistance la plus significative, à notre époque, des rapports du maître et de l'esclave'[77] (Le Guillant 1963: 912). This is hinted at in Dupré's observation on Mme Lancelin's pinching of Léa, but it is true to say that for him as for Lacan the sisters are more important as exemplars of the structuring of paranoia than as exploited human beings (or even women).

Le Guillant's narration of the killings takes it as read that the sisters were equal partners in crime ('C'est d'un même mouvement qu'elles ont massacré leurs maîtresses et se sont donné la main, chacune assurant à l'autre une part égale des violences',[78] Le Guillant 1963: 871), and promotes a view of them as conscious, not to say rational, agents of class vengeance (Christine is quoted as saying: 'Voilà assez longtemps qu'on est domestique; nous avons montré notre force',[79] Le Guillant 1963: 872).

---

[75] 'the quality and the richness of its analysis . . . it contains hardly any allusion to the fact that Christine and Léa were servants.'

[76] For an account of this debate see Roudinesco 1993: 433–5.

[77] 'the condition of being a domestic servant is the most significant survival into our day of master–slave relationships.'

[78] 'It was with one accord that they massacred their mistresses and helped each other out, each carrying out an equal share of the violence.'

[79] 'We've been servants for quite long enough; we have shown how strong we are.'

The sisters' closeness here has nothing bizarre or uncanny about it, and their crime is seen as an assertion of unity rather than, as for Lacan and Dupré, a desperate attempt to break free from it. The references provided for them by earlier employers speak glowingly of their qualities, apart from a couple which mentioned Christine's aloof, strong-headed quality. For all Le Guillant's eagerness to show parity in retribution, Christine unquestionably emerges, here as in Lessana's account, as the dominant partner, Léa even being described by M. Lancelin as her slave.

Le Guillant is not, however, a psychiatrist for nothing, and his attention, like that of Dupré after him, is soon drawn to the behavioural symptoms of 'ce qui fermentait sous l'eau dormante de l'existence des soeurs Papin dans la famille Lancelin'[80] (Le Guillant 1963: 879)—the rupture with their mother (whose name is here given as Derrée) and their visit to the town hall. His fascination with the case and with its newspaper and magazine coverage lies in the revelation they afford of 'une sorte d'accord caché entre ce crime "inexplicable" et la vie quotidienne, "banale", de deux servantes dans une famille bourgeoise du Mans en 1933'[81] (Le Guillant 1963: 891). The link between the *fait divers* and the uncanny— though Le Guillant uses neither term—is plain here. That uncanny was often recognized only partially, or even not at all, in contemporary writings on the case, Louis Martin-Chauffier's remark in *Vu* distilling it most effectively ('On voudrait comprendre: on ne peut',[82] Le Guillant 1963: 892). Le Guillant's interest, however, lies less in the psychoanalytic complexities that fascinate Lacan and Dupré than in the social and political repercussions of the case. *Le Bonhomme sarthois*, we may recall, had said: 'Personne ne peut se vanter de connaître à fond l'âme complexe des femmes et spécialement des servantes qui, chaque jour, circulent en silence autour de nous.' For Le Guillant, this invisibility of the most domesticated section of the working class is cause for scandal rather than the *frisson* it seems to procure *Le Bonhomme sarthois*'s correspondent. Servants for him are as invisible to the bourgeoisie as Alabama Blacks to Whites or 'les cadavres des "bicots" abattus'[83] (Le Guillant 1963: 897) to *pieds-noirs*. The paralleling of different modes of oppression is reminiscent of that Sartre who in September 1961, in his preface to Fanon's *Les Damnés de la terre*, had written: 'Abattre un Européen, c'est faire d'une pierre deux coups, supprimer en même temps un oppresseur

---

80 'what was fermenting beneath the sleepy waters of the Papin sisters' existence in the Lancelin household.'
81 'a kind of hidden harmony between this "inexplicable" crime and the everyday, "banal" life of two serving-girls in a 1933 Le Mans bourgeois family.'
82 'We should like to understand, but we cannot.'   83 'the corpses of murdered "wogs."'

et un'opprimé'[84] (quoted in Winock 1987: 33). It is all the more telling since he was writing immediately after the end of the Algerian war, and only two years after large numbers of Algerians living in Paris had been rounded up and thrown into the Seine by the police.

The wider context of oppression into which Le Guillant inserts the case is dramatically illustrated by his footnote reference to *La Servante criminelle*, by de Ryckere, which gives abundant examples of masters and mistresses killed or wounded by their servants. One instance quoted, from 1904, involved a maid who stabbed her mistress in the face with scissors and, to get rid of the blood, then tipped a cauldron of boiling water over her. The common denominator for all these killings is identified as 'l'esprit de vengeance'[85] (Le Guillant 1963: 896), widespread enough for a German doctor to have labelled the phenomenon 'cooks' rage', which he ascribed to the heat in which they worked. Beneath the possibly exaggerated reporting and certainly simplistic medical diagnosis, what is obvious here is the presence of an oppressed class striking back—something that was utterly disregarded alike at the trial and in Lacan's analysis. The only previous writer on the case identified by Le Guillant as giving due weight to the class factor is Gaston Chérau in *L'Écho de Paris*, who vividly evokes the inexorable build-up of tension and its repression 'jusqu-au jour où une observation tombe à faux'[86] (Le Guillant 1963: 900).

What, for Le Guillant, does the Papin case have to tell us? The sisters' exclusive closeness was fairly obviously the result of their emotionally deprived upbringing, and a mirror of that deprivation was to be found in the Lancelin family 'où Monsieur les ignorait entièrement, où Mme les commandait durement, où Mademoiselle était déjà une vieille fille'[87] (Le Guillant 1963: 907). Thus resentment transferred over from their childhood continued to fester in the rue Bruyère, eventually requiring only a single word to trigger the explosion—the word 'encore', uttered disapprovingly by Mme Lancelin on learning of the iron's repeated malfunctioning, a word that for Le Guillant was 'comme un symbole de leur état et de leur existence toute entière'[88] (Le Guillant 1963: 908). It is also, not unpleasingly, the word chosen by Lacan as the title of his most famous text (also known as *Le Séminaire XX*) on female hysteria.

---

[84] 'To strike down a European is to kill two birds with one stone, getting rid at the same time of an oppressor and one who is oppressed.'

[85] 'a spirit of vengeance.'   [86] 'until a remark/observation hits the wrong note.'

[87] 'where the master completely ignored them, the mistress gave them harsh orders, and the daughter was already an old maid.'

[88] 'like a symbol of their condition and the whole of their existence.'

'Encore' distilled the unending sameness and drudgery of the sisters' working lives, carrying with it also a suggestion of that repetition that for Freud is of the essence of Thanatos, the death drive. Le Guillant does not specifically invoke this latter point, but says in the following paragraph that 'Elle [sc. Christine] parvient à mourir'[89] (Le Guillant 1963: 909). That death, for him, was intimately linked with the misery of her social condition. At a time when (give or take the odd cleaner) the vast majority of readers of this book will have no access to domestic servants, such an interpretation may seem already outdated; but the statistics Le Guillant goes on to give provide a horrifying illustration of the wretchedness, emotional as well as material, in which so many of them lived. Suicide, successful or attempted, and internment in psychiatric institutions were far commoner for domestic servants than for other categories of the population. The Papins' bloody paranoia is compared by Le Guillant to an uprising of the colonized against their colonizers—the kind of image that was to become characteristic of much far left discourse in France after 1968. Maoist groups, of the kind with which Sartre was to sympathize, compared capitalist France to the country under Occupation, whence the name chosen by one of them (Nouvelle Résistance Populaire) and their willingness to justify individual acts of revolt or reprisal—but in France very rarely the taking of life—in the name of a greater overarching struggle. Le Guillant's assimilation of Christine and Léa is only a partial one ('On ne peut sans doute identifier—mais non plus séparer—entièrement des actes criminels isolés tel que celui des soeurs Papin à la violence des groupes sociaux opprimés',[90] Le Guillant 1963: 911), and he is aware that the Papins' criminal action was as isolated an example as it would be possible to find. But his piece makes it clear that that action can only be understood in the context of the social class to which its perpetrators belonged. The dialectic between master and slave, in which the apparently subordinate partner is in reality the stronger, was an important theme in the Hegelian Marxism by which Sartre and his entourage were heavily influenced—a view of which the Papins' killing offers a powerful illustration.

The isolation of domestic servants, with no effective organization to represent them, is the other reason adduced for the wretchedness of their condition. Genet, in *Comment jouer 'Les Bonnes'*, had been at pains to stress that his play was not a committed plea on their behalf: 'Je suppose qu'il existe un syndicat des gens de maison—cela ne nous

---

[89] 'She manages to die.'

[90] 'We cannot identify isolated criminal acts such as that of the Papin sisters with the violence of oppressed social groups, but nor can we separate the two categories entirely.'

regarde pas'[91] (Genet 1976: 10). Le Guillant's comment 'Les syndicats de "gens de maison" sont quasi virtuels'[92] is an obvious retort to Genet's slightly disdainful assertion. There appears to be a danger here of transforming the Papin sisters from victims into heroines or even role-models—something *Les Temps modernes* in its Maoist heyday a decade or so later would undoubtedly have done—but Le Guillant draws back from that in his final paragraphs:

> **Mais le pouvoir entre les mains, ils [sc. d'autres insurgés] veulent bientôt à leur tour dominer, ne tardent pas dans voir dans toute opposition 'une conjuration interne et externe', and à défendre—par tous les moyens—leur juste cause.**
>
> **N'y a-t-il pas là une menace fondamentale de toute entreprise révolutionnaire, dont il conviendrait de prendre conscience et de se garder?[93]** (Le Guillant 1963: 913)

This anticipates the stress in Michel Foucault's work from the 1970s onwards on the omnipresence of power. Foucault's target was 'not so much "such or such" an institution of power, or group, or elite, or class, but rather a technique, a form of power' (Foucault 1982: 212), which imposes itself on individuals and coerces them into particular forms of identity and subjectivity. Any 'entreprise révolutionnaire', on this reading, is menaced from within by the persistence and omnipresence of power relations, against which the supposed justice of its cause is no guarantee. This view was to become, and indeed remains, immensely influential in radical thinking throughout the West, particularly in the decay of Leninist centralism and the rise of new types of politics grounded in gender and identity. In this respect Le Guillant's warning against too hagiographic an approach towards the Papin sisters and other vengeful victims of oppression is less an old-fashioned humanist plea than a striking foreshadowing of the debates that were to characterize the decades ahead. The Papins' political awareness may have been at best minimal, but Le Guillant makes it clear that what they carried out was a political act, and one with profoundly ambiguous implications.

---

[91] 'I imagine that there is such a thing as a domestic servants' trade union, but that is no business of ours.'

[92] '"Domestic servants" trade unions scarcely exist.'

[93] 'But once power is in their hands they soon want to dominate in their turn; they are swift to see in any opposition "an internal or external conspiracy", and to defend their just cause by any and every means. Is this not a fundamental threat to any revolutionary undertaking, of which we should be aware and against which we must be vigilant?'

3 Literary Reproductions

The uniqueness of the Papin affair means that it has inspired a variety of literary reproductions in various genres, ranging from the short story to the theatre to the biographical novel, and belonging to both high and low culture. Amongst the former may be considered such well-known texts as Jean-Paul Sartre's short story *Érostrate*, Simone de Beauvoir's consideration of the affair in *La Force de l'âge*, and Jean Genet's play *Les Bonnes*. Less well known than these texts, but important in its own right, is Wendy Kesselman's play *Sister my Sister*, whose success helped to promote the affair in the area of gender studies, especially in the United States. Paulette Houdyer's biographical novel, *L'Affaire Papin*, a 'factional' account of the lives of the sisters, has ensured that the case continues to reach a wider audience, belonging as it does to popular culture. The same can be said of Le Texier's novel, *Les Soeurs Papin*, which is a kind of spin on the *polar* (detective novel). These different accounts all help to add to our understanding of the affair, and in turn the affair may at times be said to shed new light on various aspects of the writers' thoughts and preoccupations. It is with this in mind that we intend to explore the texts in this chapter, beginning with the Surrealists for whom the Papin sisters constituted a veritable icon.

The Surrealists and wayward women

The Surrealists were the first to put the Papin sisters on the literary map in a short piece written by Paul Eluard and Benjamin Péret which appeared in *Le Surréalisme au service de la révolution* (1933), along with the sisters' 'before' picture and the Surrealists' *photomontage* of the sisters 'after' the killings. The killings were perfect grist to the Surrealist mill since they embodied an act of revolt against the established order, striking as they did at the very heart of bourgeois society.

The Surrealists, whose revolutionary members were both writers and artists, were dedicated to undermining the status quo both politically and artistically. Their aims were set out by André Breton in the *Manifeste du Surréalisme* (1924) and developed in the *Second Manifeste du*

Surréalisme (1930). They sought to liberate literature and art from the narrow confines of realism by drawing on the unconscious and on dream imagery, and this resulted in experiments in automatic writing and in the juxtaposition of incongruous images, combining reality and dreams, in literary texts and in painting. Their debt to Freudian psychoanalysis is clear and indeed, as Macey points out, they viewed Freud as 'an ally in their attack on the bourgeoisie and all its works', since his theories questioned prevalent notions of mental health (1988: 60). In doing away with the line existing between so-called normality and abnormality, Freud paved the way for the premiss in Breton's *Nadja* (1928) that there is no definite divide between madness and sanity. *Nadja* also saw the first reference to 'convulsive beauty', later elaborated in *L'Amour fou* (1937), which is experienced in terms of a 'frisson', a mixture of eroticism and terror. As Macey asserts, 'in the summer of 1933, convulsive beauty is made flesh by three killers: Violette Nozières and the Papin sisters' (67). The Papin sisters, along with Violette Nozières, who killed her father at the time of the Papin trial and to whom the Surrealists dedicated a book, belong to a series of delinquent women celebrated by the Surrealists. Their number includes Germaine Berton, who assassinated the Action Française leader Maurice Plateau in 1923, and Marguerite Pantaine, the 'Aimée' of Lacan's thesis, who tried to kill the well-known actress Huguette Duflos in 1931.

What is particularly interesting about Eluard and Péret's text on the Papin sisters is its positioning within the journal as a whole. It lies adjacent to an article by Paul Nougé entitled 'Les Images défendues' on the nature of sight and the role of metaphor in art, and is immediately followed by René Magritte's, *Vierge retroussée* ('retroussée' meaning 'hitched up', because the 'Virgin's' skirt is hitched up around her thighs). Nougé's deliberation on sight is clearly relevant given that both the Lancelins had their eyes plucked out. As for Magritte's illustration, its position ensures that it acts as a commentary on the killings and vice versa as Christopher Lane (1993) has pointed out. The *Vierge retroussée* depicts the figure of a nun in full habit with a halo above her head, which sharply contrasts with the fact that she is winking and lifting the skirt of her habit to reveal high heels, stockings, suspenders, and a slip beneath. In fact, one might go as far as to say that the nun condenses into pictorial form the intended 'meaning' of the Papin text, which in turn condenses the lives of the sisters into three short paragraphs:

Les soeurs Papin furent élevées au couvent du Mans. Puis leur mère les plaça dans une maison 'bourgeoise' de cette ville. Six ans, elles endurèrent avec la plus parfaite soumission observations, exigences, injures. La crainte, la

fatigue, l'humiliation, enfantaient lentement en elles la haine, cet alcool très .
doux qui console en secret car il promet à la violence de lui adjoindre, tôt ou
tard, la force physique.

    Le jour venu, Léa et Christine Papin rendirent sa monnaie au mal, une
monnaie de fer rouge. Elles massacrèrent littéralement leurs patronnes, leur
arrachant les yeux, leur écrasant la tête. Puis elles se lavèrent soigneusement
et, délivrées, indifférentes, se couchèrent. La foudre était tombée, le bois
brûlé, le soleil définitivement éteint.

    Sorties tout armées d'un chant de Maldoror . . .[1]

    What is immediately apparent is the absence of any explicit reference
in the text to the surmised sexual relationship between the sisters.
However, sexuality is clearly supplied by the *Vierge retroussée* which
represents a stereotypical heterosexual fantasy figure (Lane 1993) and
not the homoerotic figure one might expect. This, of course, helps to
highlight the extent to which the events of the lives of the sisters
are reduced and reworked to fit the Surrealist project. In terms of
nomenclature, the sisters are clearly equated with the nun for the
nun is a 'bonne soeur' and the women are both 'soeurs' (sisters) and
'bonnes' (maids), who were, initially at any rate, 'bonnes' (good). The
text immediately takes up the image of the nun, in that it ignores
other aspects of the sisters' background and focuses instead on their
convent upbringing. It goes on to say that their mother then placed
them in a 'bourgeois' household—the quotation marks suggesting that
the word should take on its full connotations—where they underwent
terrible hardship (the notes from the trial, however, suggest that the
household in which the sisters worked was no better or worse than
many others of the time) and it is because of this, according to Eluard
and Péret, that they eventually turned to violence. The nun reminds us
that appearances can be deceptive: the maids might have had a convent
upbringing but beneath the surface subversive forces are lurking.
The metaphor of 'alcool' or spirit employed to signify the hatred which
builds up in the sisters also plays a double role: it evokes the violence
contained in the 'drinking classes' such as in Zola's *L'Assommoir* (1887)
for instance, and paradoxically it takes up the idea of the spiritual

---

[1] 'The Papin sisters were brought up in a convent in Le Mans. Then their mother placed them in a
"bourgeois" household in that town. For six years, they endured observations, demands, insults with
the most perfect patience. Fear, fatigue, humiliation slowly gave birth to hatred, that very sweet
alcohol which consoles in secret because it promises to add, sooner or later, physical force to violence. Came the day when Léa and Christine Papin paid evil back its dues in currency of red-hot
iron. They literally massacred their employers, tearing out their eyes and smashing in their heads.
Then they washed themselves carefully and, delivered, indifferent, went to bed. The thunderbolt
had struck, the wood had burned, the sun had gone out for good. They emerged fully armed from
a song of Maldoror . . .'

contained in the image of the *Vierge retroussée*. What consoles 'en secret' (in secret) is what lurks beneath the habit or surface: an erotic image on the one hand, physical violence on the other. Or rather both at once, for sex and violence are conflated: the positioning of the image of the nun means that what is violent in the women's action is necessarily erotic, and, by the same token, what is erotic is also violent. This of course evokes another of the Surrealists' favourite images: that of the 'mante religieuse' (praying mantis) which devours its mate once the sexual act is completed. At any rate, what lurks beneath the exterior of both maids and nun is dangerous: the one attacks the bourgoisie, the other the Catholic church, which for the Surrealists constitute the two main power-bearing institutions in society. Catholicism barely hides its sexual hypocrisy says the nun (Lane 1993), just as the bourgeoisie barely hides its well-to-do hypocrisy in the harsh treatment of the maids which provokes their violence.

What clearly emerges from the Surrealists' text is their attitude towards women. Females are targeted here as part of the status quo: the nuns responsible for the sisters' upbringing; the mistresses in the 'bourgeois' household; and the mother of the girls for placing them in this household. The review therefore betrays not only a championing of the female in the shape of the maids and the nun, in that they are liberating figures who will act against a social order which is repressive and corrupt, but also a fear of the power of women and of female sexuality in particular. An initial response to the lines of the Nougé text which are set beside the *Vierge retroussée* might be said to justify the former view. It reads: 'Le refus de l'ordre établi, la volonté de ruiner les valeurs en cours ou d'en introduire de nouvelles, l'intention subversive essentielle se doivent servir de tous les moyens, au gré des circonstances'[2] (Nougé 1933: 28). However, one could argue that the *Vierge retroussée*, far from being a subversive attack on the established order, simply reproduces what has been the prevalent male view of women throughout the ages in that it amalgamates in one image the virgin/whore dichotomy and in so doing betrays the ambiguous feelings on the part of the Surrealists towards women which many critics have noted (Gauthier 1971; Chadwick 1985).

The metaphor used to explain the maids' violent action is based on monetary exchange. Evil is given its dues in currency of red-hot iron. Here the text is obviously referring to the iron which blew the fuse in the Lancelin household and precipitated the events that led to the murders.

---

[2] 'Refusal of the established order, the will to ruin current values or to introduce new ones, essential subversive intention, must employ all means available according to circumstance.'

Reference to the iron also conjures up images of what must have been used to bludgeon the skulls of the mistresses (indeed in Papatakis's film, *Les Abysses*, an iron is used precisely to that effect). What is 'evil' is clearly the 'patronnes'—employers and 'owners' of the girls. As for the portrayal of the deed itself, the text concentrates on the tearing out of the eyes and the smashing in of the heads of the mistresses. This is not surprising given the Surrealist preoccupation with eyes and sight. Once again the importance of the Nougé article comes into play as does the image which opens the Buñuel and Dali film, *Un Chien andalou* (1928), which in its opening sequences depicts a woman's eye being split open by a sharpened razor. Here the Papin sisters dare to carry out (and with their bare hands) what the Surrealists only dreamt of on film. This, in turn, refers us back to the nun who is winking and whose left eye therefore simply appears as a slit.

Having described the murders, the text then returns to religious imagery: after the massacre the sisters cleanse themselves and, freed or delivered (from evil—with its resonances of the Lord's Prayer), and indifferent, go to bed. The fact that they were found in bed together (although the text is ambiguous on this point; 'se couchèrent' can simply mean that they went to bed, not necessarily together), once again brings us back to the sexually subversive image of the nun. The final sentence of the paragraph refers us to an almost supernatural power in the thunderbolt which has struck, the wood which has burned, and the sun which has been extinguished (divine justice in the form of the sisters' actions has triumphed, the established order has crumbled, and the sun has been extinguished especially for the two mistresses, whose eyes have been put out). The image here of the 'soleil noir' comes to mind in the work of Nerval and Van Gogh.

The passage ends with the image of the sisters emerging fully armed from one of the *Chants de Maldoror* (1874), Lautréamont's poetic work and one of the Surrealists' favourite texts, the eponymous hero of which is a Satanic figure who pits himself against God. This gives the action poetic force, lifting it from the realms of everyday social reality and promoting it to the realms of the literary. If for David Macey, the sisters thus signify 'convulsive beauty made flesh' (1988: 67), for the likes of Nicole Ward Jouve, the Lautréamont analogy simply implies a male appropriation of a female act. She asks:

Does that mean that through the act of killing women become men—that a nobler, a revolutionary, male and poetic self is thus born? Does this further imply that women as women cannot emancipate themselves, cannot kill? It certainly looks as if Breton and Péret through this passage and through the montage, were recuperating what they saw as the poetic charge of the deed for themselves, young men such as themselves. (Ward Jouve 1998: 70)

Leaving aside the rather curious equation of emancipation and killing, Ward Jouve does have a point. But once again the Surrealist position is somewhat ambivalent. On the one hand yes, it does seem that they have appropriated the deed for themselves, on the other, the *Vierge retroussée* which immediately follows the article suggests that the 'femaleness' of the deed is kept firmly in mind, with all the ambivalence that that entails. It also reminds us, and men in particular, that female sexuality is ultimately dangerous: you might end up losing your eyes (since Freud a synonym for the testes and a parallel exploited by Georges Bataille in his *Histoire de l'oeil*).

There is also a sense in which the 'before' and 'after' photographs reproduce the *Vierge retroussée*: above is the image of the 'sages filles' (sensible girls), below is that of the harpies lurking under the surface. As Ward Jouve rightly says, following Sartre, it is impossible to look at the photographs without thinking of the crime which separates them. What the Surrealist text does is fill in the gap which exists between 'before' and 'after'. The 'after' picture illustrates what the maids have become once the crime has been committed, indeed the caption of the *photomontage* reads: *Sorties tout armées d'un chant de Maldoror*,[3] thus reproducing the last line of Péret and Eluard's text.

One might even go as far as to say that the Surrealist text grew out of the *photomontage* which was in turn produced in response to reports of the case. For what is immediately interesting in the second paragraph is that the text refers to Léa and Christine rather than the other way round. Given that Christine was the elder sister and Léa simply followed her example, the trial notes and the journalistic reports tend to refer to Christine first. In the 'before' picture Christine is on the left facing us, whilst in the 'after' *photomontage*, Léa is on the left, the *montage* having inverted the original image. The Surrealists therefore appear to have 'read' their own image from left to right as they would a written text and their reading resulted in the text in the review.

The photographs have come to stand for the crime itself in much the same way as the well-known picture of Myra Hindley has come to signify the Moors murders. Indeed, the photographs of the Papin sisters are at the centre of many reproductions of the case including those by Sartre and Beauvoir.

[3]   *They emerged fully armed from a song of Maldoror.*

Jean-Paul Sartre's *Érostrate*

Written in 1936, *Érostrate* was published in 1939 in the collection of short stories *Le Mur*. The text is about Paul Hilbert, an anti-humanist, who decides that he will commit the ultimate free action: a crime with no motive. He will shoot five people for the sake of it and use the sixth bullet on himself. The narrative has been interpreted in two main ways: either Hilbert is an existentialist anti-hero, or he is a deluded character prey to acute paranoia and angst of a psychological rather than existential nature. Hilbert, who is clearly a precursor of Roquentin in *La Nausée* (1939), has a number of diegetic and non-diegetic models. Ronald Hayman informs us that he is partly based on one of Sartre's students, Didelot, who was 'brilliant, illegitimate, depressive and fascistic' and who cut his throat one morning with two razor blades before running to the roof top and jumping off shouting to passers by to get out of the way as he did so (1986: 113). Others have noted Hilbert's resemblance to Jean Genet, the self-styled homosexual criminal whose play *Les Bonnes* (1947), draws on the Papin sisters and about whom Sartre wrote an existential analysis entitled *Saint Genet, comédien et martyr* (1971–2). Others still have pointed out that he is a mixture of Lautréamont's Maldoror and Gide's Lafcadio, both of whom are advocates of the 'acte gratuit', which, in its simplest form for the Surrealists, consists in going out on to the street and firing into the crowd. The diegetic models are Herostratus who burned down the Temple at Ephesus, one of the seven wonders of the ancient world and dedicated to the goddess Diana, for no other reason than he wanted to become famous, and the Papin sisters upon whose 'before' and 'after' pictures Hilbert muses as he looks at himself in the mirror.

The text therefore draws on a number of cultural references (taken from real life and from literature) and in juxtaposing Herostratus and the Papin sisters it aims, in the first instance, as in the Surrealist account, at attacking the two mainstay institutions of French society at the time of writing: the church (although displaced here to the temple of a previous culture) and the bourgeoisie.

That Sartre has the Papin sisters in mind from early on in his narrative is made clear by the fact that the prostitute Hilbert visits on a regular basis is called Léa. Indeed, a parallel can be drawn between the Papins' homoerotic relationship and Hilbert's relationship with Léa, and later with the Léa-substitute, the older Renée. For whilst Gary Woodle asserts that 'conspicuous by its absence is any indication of the latent homo-sexuality (or even fear of it, or confusion of sexual identity) intrinsic to

Freud's formulation of paranoiogenesis' (1974: 31), Jean Bellemin-Noël is at pains to establish the opposite. In his 'Le Diamant noir: échographie d'*Érostrate*', he points to Josette Pacaly's *Sartre au miroir* in which she reads *Érostrate* in relation to Sartre's *Saint Genet*, Genet's *Les Bonnes*, and Lacan's article on the Papin sisters. He sums up Pacaly's portrait of Hilbert thus:

> **Paul Hilbert ne peut haïr qu'un homme, objet d'amour refusé et transmué en persécuteur; il rêve d'exploser comme un pénis devenu bombe ou revolver; il souhaite d'être agressé par des hommes; sa phobie du contact est l'envers d'un désir de palper les corps masculins; le plaisir solitaire, enfin, est le seul qu'il connaisse parce qu'il craint une relation à l'autre où la castration viendrait menacer son intégrité.[4] (1986: 72)**

Hilbert tells us that he has never had intimate relations with women because 'elles vous dévorent le bas-ventre avec leur grande bouche poilue'[5] (84), which indicates his fear of woman as castrator. With Léa he assumes the role of voyeur and simply watches without touching. His fear of castration is again stressed by his loss of consciousness on seeing a dead man in the street who has fallen on his nose. The man has lost his symbolic phallus and has been left with a bloody wound instead. Not only has he been castrated but he has, in Freudian terms, also become a woman (Bellemin-Noël 1986). Hilbert's fear of women here is paralleled by his fear of becoming like a woman, that is to say penetrated by men, which, in turn, disguises his wish to be sodomized. Hilbert's open fear and dislike of women and their anatomy (he humiliates the older Renée by making her parade around naked in front of him while he waves his revolver at her), added to his paranoia and 'homophobia'—in the primal sense of the word since he is an anti-humanist and claims that he hates men—lay bare his latent homosexuality.

Like the Papin sisters, or at least as they emerge in Lacan's text, Hilbert will perpetrate a crime against those who reflect back to him his own desires. For him, the sisters' perfect crime can be read in their faces, in the 'before' and 'after' photographs (again, it is as if those interested in the case have to turn to the photographs since they constitute what is most tangible about an event which had no witnesses). Here the photographs not only reproduce graphically the events of the

---

[4] 'Paul Hilbert can only hate a man, an object of love which has been rejected and transmuted into a persecutor; he dreams of exploding like a penis which has become a bomb or revolver; he wants to be manhandled by men; his fear of being touched is the inverse of a desire to feel up male bodies; finally, solitary pleasure is all he knows because he fears a relation with the other in which castration would menace his integrity.'

[5] 'they devour your lower belly with their large hairy mouths.'

crime and the trial which follows but point to other reproductions of the affair.

The theme of sex and violence which was apparent in the Surrealist text is also pursued when Hilbert describes the sisters' faces in the 'before' photograph: 'Avant, leurs visages se balançaient comme des fleurs sages au-dessus de cols de piqué'[6] (95). This not only gives them an about-to-be-picked feel, thus conjuring up the image of the guillotine to which Christine was initially condemned, but also gives the impression that having their heads chopped off would, to extend the metaphor, somehow deflower them. This violent action on the part of the State is therefore eroticized to assume the role of a type of sexual initiation-cum-castration.

We are also told that the sisters 'respiraient l'hygiène et l'honnêteté appétisante'[7] (95)—which of course is full of irony given Hilbert's dislike of such 'honnêtes gens'. He goes on: 'Un fer discret avait ondulé pareillement leurs cheveux.'[8] Again there is obviously an allusion here to the iron which blew the fuse in the Lancelin household. The passage continues: 'Plus rassurante encore que leurs cheveux frisés, que leurs cols et que leur air d'être en visite chez le photographe, il y avait leur ressemblance de soeurs, leur ressemblance si bien pensante, qui mettait tout de suite en avant les liens du sang et les racines naturelles du groupe familial'[9] (95). This passage is again thick with irony, Hilbert, and his creator Sartre, both hating the ideology and the bourgeois order of the family (Ward Jouve 1998: 71). The visit to the photographer which Hilbert mentions is more explicitly exploited by Wendy Kesselman in *My Sister in this House* (1982) and later by Nancy Meckler in *Sister my Sister* (1994) which provide us with the background of how the 'before' photographs reproduced in so many newspapers came about.

Having analysed the 'before' pictures, Hilbert then turns to the 'after' pictures. His remark, 'après, leurs faces resplendissaient comme des incendies' (after, their faces were radiant like fires), recalls not only the surrealist text which states that after the event 'le bois avait brûlé',[10] but also the fire with which Herostratus destroyed the temple. Hilbert also lays stress on the eyes in particular knowing full well, as Ward Jouve points out, 'what these women did to other women's eyes' (1998: 71). In

---

[6] 'Before, their faces floated like wise flowers above starched collars.'
[7] 'radiated hygiene and appetising honesty.'
[8] 'A discreet iron had waved their hair in a similar way.'
[9] 'Still more reassuring than their wavy hair, their collars and their air of being at the photographers, was their likeness as sisters, a right-thinking likeness, which foregrounded at once blood ties and the natural roots of the family group.'
[10] 'the wood had burned.'

referring to the sisters' eyes, therefore, he is recalling the sexual tensions which existed in the Lancelin household as well as Lacan's view that the sisters plucked out their mistresses' eyes as the Bacchae castrated, an image which is reiterated when he imagines the police putting out one of his eyes. The image of the guillotine here is also made explicit: 'Elles avaient le cou nu des futures décapitées'[11] (95). The flowers in the 'before' picture are certainly going to be picked and in losing their heads the sisters will be deflowered. The portrait continues: 'Des rides partout, d'horribles rides de peur et de haine, des plis, des trous dans la chair comme si une bête avec des griffes avait tourné en rond sur leurs visages'[12] (95). The mention of 'bête' (beast) of course throws us back to the idea of the 'brebis enragées' (enraged ewes) in the journalistic reports and forward to Beauvoir's text which draws attention to this metaphor. And as Ward Jouve rightly remarks, 'it is as if [Hilbert] projected the hurt that the sisters inflicted on their victims on to the "after" faces'. She goes on: 'I cannot see those holes and wrinkles he describes' (1998: 71). However, she should not be surprised, for Sartre is merely using poetic licence for his own puposes in much the same way as the Surrealists did in their *photomontage* of the Papin sisters in which, as Ward Jouve herself humorously points out, Christine looks uncannily like André Breton! (70).

What Sartre's version of the 'after' photographs does is make the crime itself more 'visible' to the reader in the faces of the women. Perhaps there is also a sense in which Sartre is commenting on the way in which the real 'after' photographs do not in fact point to the crime as they came to once the press took charge of them (however, there is also a point to be made here which still holds true today: we still rely heavily on physiognomy as an indicator of character in an almost Dickensian fashion). Not only have the sisters changed beyond recognition in *Érostrate*, they also no longer look alike. Hilbert goes on to say: 'Elles ne se ressemblaient plus. Chacune portait à sa manière le souvenir de leur crime commun.'[13] In a sense, their crime has freed them from the bonds of bourgeois society and the tyranny of its ideology and the sisters have now become individuals in their own right. Hilbert hopes for an even greater transformation. As Woodle points out he not only wants 'an individuality that will cut him off from the human family altogether', but 'his effort is to

---

[11] 'They had the bare necks of those who were going to be beheaded.'
[12] 'Wrinkles everywhere, horrible wrinkles of fear and hatred, furrows, holes in the flesh as if a beast with claws had drawn circles on their faces.'
[13] 'They no longer resembled each other. They each bore the memory of their common crime in their own way.'

bring about, if only for an instant, the coincidence or fusion of the Hero with his Act, of consciousness with the Self, of Existence with Being' (1974: 34–5).

Of course, he is doomed to failure because if Hilbert's interpretation significantly ignores the psychological reasons behind the Papins' behaviour (for him they act purely out of free will), Sartre's does not. Whereas for the Surrealists the simplest act is to fire into a crowd at random, for Hilbert this is far from simple and he finds he cannot shoot. When he eventually does shoot, it is to prevent himself from crying out in response to a man holding out his hand towards the gun that Hilbert is pointing at him (and in a sense this could be construed as sexual exchange). He only definitely kills one person and maybe wounds two others when he fires at the people chasing him. Hilbert now becomes the victim; the crime of the Papin sisters will be visited upon his own physique by the police whom he thinks will beat him, if they capture him, which they eventually do: 'S'ils me prennent ils vont me battre, me casser des dents, ils me crèveront peut-être un oeil'[14] (102). His fear of castration here is matched only by his subconscious desire for anal intercourse—the anus, as Bataille demonstrates, is a blind eye. Hilbert's desire eventually overcomes his fear in that he opens the door of the toilet in which he has been hiding and gives himself up. If the Papins, within the context of *Érostrate*, break free of society, Hilbert is ultimately reintegrated.

Simone de Beauvoir and the *fait divers*

In the second volume of her autobiography, *La Force de l'âge* (1960), Simone de Beauvoir writes about her own and Sartre's reaction to the Papin affair when it appeared in the press of 1933. Her piece is interesting not least because she was only the second woman after Janet Flanner to have responded to the case. Writing almost thirty years later, she also has the advantage of hindsight and examines the Papin affair in a way which is both self-conscious and sometimes ironic and which therefore highlights the ambivalence which underpins her and Sartre's feelings about the case. As a result, Beauvoir not only throws light on the Papin affair, but, by a reciprocal action, the Papin case helps to facilitate an understanding of her and Sartre's intellectual stance at the time.

---

[14] 'If they catch me they will beat me, smash my teeth in, perhaps gouge out one of my eyes.'

At the time that the murders took place and during the trial that followed, Beauvoir tells us that she and Sartre had teaching posts in Rouen and Le Havre respectively and used to visit each other as often as possible. They were preoccupied with trying to understand what determined people's behaviour and the choices they made. Lacking a sufficient number of acquaintances to analyse, they turned to the *fait divers* in newspapers and in magazines such as *Détective* for examples of extreme behaviour which highlighted passions common to so-called 'normal' people and which differed in these accounts only in degree rather than in kind. With regard to methodology, both Sartre and Beauvoir were wary of classical psychoanalysis. Beauvoir asserts: 'Nous reprochions aux psychanalystes de décomposer l'homme plutôt de le comprendre. L'application quasi automatique de leurs clés leur servait à rationaliser fallacieusement des expériences qu'il aurait fallu appréhender dans leur singularité'[15] (1960: 147). It was largely as a result of this that Sartre invented the concept of 'mauvaise foi' (dishonesty or self-deception) to account for behaviour which others attributed to the unconscious such as 'tricheries du langage, mensonges de la mémoire, fuites, compensations, sublimations'[16] (1960: 148).

Their denial of the unconscious, however, was not as absolute as this might suggest. And here Beauvoir points to one of the main contradictions which existed in her and Sartre's thinking at the time:

> Une de nos contradictions, c'est que nous niions l'inconscient; cependant Gide, les surréalistes et, malgré nos résistances, Freud lui-même, nous avaient convaincus qu'il existe en tout être un 'infracassable noyau de nuit' [Breton]: quelque chose qui ne réussit à percer ni les routines sociales ni les lieux commun du langage mais qui parfois éclate, scandaleusement. Dans ces explosions, toujours une vérité se révèle, et nous trouvions bouleversantes celles qui délivrent une liberté.[17] (1960: 149–50)

So their interest in the Papin affair clearly arose at a time when Beauvoir and Sartre were trying to negotiate their own position *vis-à-vis* the unconscious. The ambivalence in their thinking is stressed by the

---

[15] 'We reproached the psychoanalysts for pulling man apart rather than understanding him. Applying their keys more or less automatically allowed them to rationalize falsely experiences which ought to have been understood in their singularity.'

[16] 'tricks of language, faults in memory, evasiveness, compensations, sublimations.'

[17] 'One of the contradictions is that we denied the existence of the unconscious; however, Gide, the surrealists and, despite our resistance, Freud himself, convinced us that there exists in every being "an unbreakable kernel of darkness": something which succeeds in piercing neither social routine nor the commonplaces of language but which sometimes explodes scandalously. In these explosions, a fundamental truth is always revealed, and we were overwhelmed by those which set liberty free.'

fact that Beauvoir hints that the key to the Papin affair perhaps lies within this 'infracassable noyau de nuit' ('unbreakable kernel of darkness'), which one day exploded and resulted in the killings which, in turn, revealed a fundamental truth: that society was to blame (Kamenish 1996: 99).

In a passage which is not devoid of irony, Beauvoir explains that whilst they often failed to look below the surface of cases which were signifi- cant in terms of the psychology of the individual, she and Sartre were quick to get to the bottom of things when it came to class issues. It is for this reason, says Beauvoir, that they immediately understood what she refers to as 'la tragédie des soeurs Papin' ('the tragedy of the Papin sisters'). Like Violette Nozières who was convicted of parricide at the time of the Papin trial, the sisters were essentially victims. Beauvoir writes:

> Dans ses grandes lignes, la tragédie des soeurs Papin nous fut tout de suite intelligible. A Rouen, comme au Mans, et peut-être même parmi les mères de mes élèves, il y avait certainement de ces femmes qui retiennent sur les gages de leur bonne le prix d'une assiette cassée, qui enfilent des gants blancs pour déceler sur les meubles des grains de poussière oubliés: à nos yeux, elles méri- taient cent fois la mort.[18] (1960: 151)

For Ward Jouve, Beauvoir constitutes 'a lone voice, and one that seems to arise from a gender experience—not just a female experience of domesticity, but identifying with the killers as daughters against the mothers. It is a point of entry which the male commentators of the period seem to be lacking' (Ward Jouve 1998: 66). It is thus Beauvoir's situation as a woman, as much as her political stance, which makes her able to appreciate why the crime took place. She goes on to comment:

> Avec leurs cheveux ondulés et leurs collerettes blanches, que Christine et Léa semblaient sages, sur l'ancienne photo que publièrent certains journaux! Comment étaient-elles devenues ces furies hagardes qu'offraient à la vindicte publique des clichés pris après le drame? Il fallait en rendre responsable l'orphelinat de leur enfance, leur servage, tout cet affreux système à fabri- quer des fous, des assassins, des monstres qu'ont agencé les gens de bien. L'horreur de cette machine broyeuse ne pouvait être équitablement dénon- cée que par une horreur exemplaire: les deux soeurs s'étaient faites les in- struments et les martyres d'une sombre justice.[19] (1960: 151)

---

[18] 'Broadly speaking, the tragedy of the Papin sisters was immediately understandable to us. In Rouen, as in Le Mans, and perhaps even among the mothers of my students, there were certainly women who took the price of a broken plate out of their maid's wages, who put on white gloves to reveal forgotten specks of dust on the furniture: in our eyes, they deserved to die a hundred times over.'

[19] 'With their wavy hair and their white collars, how sensible Christine and Léa looked in the old photo that some newspapers published! How had they become these haggard furies which the

Like the Surrealists and Sartre, Beauvoir's response to the killings is also determined by the 'before' and 'after' pictures which appeared in the press. The force which turned the 'sages filles' ('sensible girls') of the 'before' picture into the 'furies hagardes' ('haggard furies') of the 'after' pictures is deemed to be society itself. What is surprising, however, is that Beauvoir, despite her gendered position, does not question the validity of the pictures which are clearly constructs of the male gaze and products of the very society she is condemning. What she does draw attention to, however, is that both she and Sartre were as guilty as the psychoanalysts whom they accused of using the same criteria to understand every event. Their initial understanding of the Papin case was based on their own preconceptions of class: the maids were justified in killing their employers and their act was essentially one of rebellion. However, upon reading the reviews of the trial they had to concede that:

> **Indéniablement, l'aînée était atteinte d'une paranoïa aiguë, et la cadette épousait son délire. Nous avions donc eu tort de voir dans leurs excès le sauvage déchaînement d'une liberté; elles avaient frappé plus ou moins à l'aveuglette, à travers des terreurs confuses; nous répugnions à le croire et nous continuâmes sourdement à les admirer.[20] (1960: 151)**

The vocabulary here is loaded and draws attention to the sisters' sexual relationship in the use of 'épousait' ('espoused') and to the ripping out of their mistresses' eyes in the reference to their action as being carried out 'à l'aveuglette' ('blindly'). It is also here that Breton's 'infraccasable noyau de nuit' ('unbreakable kernel of darkness') comes into play once more but no liberating experience is forthcoming. What is noticeable here is that Beauvoir and Sartre are so blinded by their own beliefs that they do not want to believe the evidence confronting them, although they were nevertheless frustrated when the psychiatrists attached to the case found that the sisters were of sound mind. Eventually they both had to admit that Christine was mentally unstable, when two days after being sentenced to death, she had to be put in a straitjacket and incarcerated in an asylum. Beauvoir comments: 'Si la maladie

---

photos taken after the drama exposed to public condemnation? The responsibility for this surely lay with their "orphaned" childhood, their servitude, the whole of this dreadful system put in place by the well-to-do which fabricates mad people, killers, monsters. The horror of this grinding machine could only be fairly denounced by an exemplary horror: the sisters had made themselves into the instruments and the martyrs of a sombre justice.'

[20] 'Undeniably, the elder sister suffered from acute paranoia, and the younger one espoused her delirium. We had therefore been wrong to see the wild unleashing of freedom in their excesses; they hit out more or less blindly, in confused terror; we were loath to believe it and we quietly continued to admire them.'

de Christine ternissait un peu son crime, l'indignité des jurés en était multipliée'[21] (1960: 151).

Christopher Lane (1993) rightly points out that Beauvoir and Sartre were as guilty as the jury who refused to take the sisters' diminished mental state into account, in that they both saw Christine's delirium as tarnishing the crime. He asserts: 'The irony is that Beauvoir repeated the same procedure by making Christine's "malady" an unfortunate presence that "tarnished her crime" because it diminished her political and rebellious worth . . . For what is more obviously tarnished is Beauvoir's attempt to recuperate the crime for an existential significance' (1993: 51–2).

However, if they were wrong about the sisters, they felt they were still right about society and derived some pleasure from this. Beauvoir simply turns away from the crime itself to the verdict of the jury and presides over the jurors instead so that she is able to use the outcome of the trial for her own purposes. She and Sartre go on to draw conclusions about society as a whole. She asserts:

> **Nous nous plaisions à constater que notre société n'était pas plus éclairée que celles qu'elle appelle 'primitives'; si elle avait posé entre le crime et le criminel un rapport de causalité, elle eût conclu à l'irresponsabilité de Gorguloff et des soeurs Papin; en fait, elle établissait un lien de 'participation' entre le meurtre et son objet: pour un Président de la République abattu, pour deux bourgeoises mises en pièces, il fallait *a priori* et en tout cas une expiation sanglante; l'assassin n'était pas jugé: il servait de bouc émissaire.[22] (1960: 152)**

What is interesting here is that Beauvoir accords the same significance to the Papin murders as she does to the assassination of President Doumer in 1932 by Gorguloff who was publicly executed for his crime. For Beauvoir, killing two women of the bourgeoisie is a similar offence in that it attacks the foundations of society. Furthermore, in turning her attention from the perpetrators of the crime to the dispensers of justice, Beauvoir puts the latter on trial instead. It is here that Lacan's 'an eye for an eye' can be seen to come into play once more. It is not the sisters who

---

[21] 'If Christine's illness tarnished her crime somewhat, the unworthiness of the jury was multiplied by it.'

[22] 'It gave us pleasure to establish that our society was no more enlightened than those which it dubs "primitive"; if it had established a causal relationship between the crime and the criminal, it would have concluded that Gorguloff and the Papin sisters were not responsible for their actions; in fact, society established a "participatory" link between the murder and its object: for a murdered President of the Republic, for two bourgeois women who had been hacked to pieces, it was necessary *a priori* and in any case to have a bloody atonement; the assassin wasn't judged: he served as a scapegoat.'

are applying the literal 'eye for eye' formula but society who, in condemning Christine to death, is demanding 'an eye for an eye' in the figurative and biblical sense.

In assessing the affair, Beauvoir begins with an indictment of society, moves on to a seeming acceptance of the psychological reasons behind the sisters' behaviour, and ends up by condemning society for the criminal way in which it treats its criminals. Lane goes as far as to argue that:

> Psychosis brought existentialism to a conceptual halt by unsettling—and even violating—deliberate and established elements of consciousness. From her initial distrust of the discipline to a period of temporary acceptance, Beauvoir finally discarded psychoanalysis. For after describing the Papin affair in terms that seemed inadequate to the trauma of the sisters, Beauvoir decided to close the episode by a hasty and unpredictable shift to sexology and the work of Magnus Hirschfield. (1993: 52)

If Lane is disappointed by the fact that the Papin case had no lasting effect on the views of Beauvoir and Sartre with regard to psychoanalysis, for Kamenish, Beauvoir's text has wider implications in that it highlights the ways in which crime and punishment were (and we might add to some extent still are) meted out in French and, by extension, capitalist society. Kamenish asserts:

> In fact, Beauvoir posits certain ideas about madness, crime, and punishment that are later taken up by Michel Foucault in his 1975 *Surveiller et punir: naissance de la prison*, as well as his 1961 *Folie et déraison*. The antiquated system of public punishment based on pain and spectacle, although theoretically rejected more than a century before the Papin affair, was revived in the very public trial of Christine and Léa by virtue of an overzealous press spurred on by the demands of the reading populace. (1996: 101)

Beauvoir's text on the Papin sisters, therefore, short as it may be, has implications which go well beyond the actual case and which contains the seeds of discourses which come to prominence in the future including a more gendered approach to female violence and the ways in which such violence is dealt with in the society in which we live.

Jean Genet's *Les Bonnes*

The best-known work inspired by the Papin case is without doubt *Les Bonnes*, by Jean Genet, first performed and published in 1947. We shall obviously not have space here for a thorough exegesis of the play

(Magedera, 1998, is a useful introduction to it and provides a valuable bibliography), but shall be focusing on it, and the texts it in its turn inspired, as one in a series of reworkings or reproductions of the Papin affair. Genet is among the most striking examples of the *écrivain maudit*, marginal and controversial in his life and his work alike. Illegitimate, never knowing who his father was, abandoned by his mother, given to running away from the age of 13, he spent much of his adolescence and early adulthood in young offenders' institutions or deserting from the army. Until the age of 34 he lived essentially by stealing and homosexual prostitution—two important themes in his autobiographical novel *Journal du voleur/The Thief's Journal*. Cocteau and Sartre were enthusiastic about his work and succeeded in getting him released from prison on a presidential pardon in 1949. Thenceforth he was a major figure in French writing, producing poetry and political texts as well as drama and fiction. But he was unhappy with the absorption of his work into the cultural establishment, an unhappiness that caused him to abjure fiction (much as Sartre for different reasons had done before) in 1952 and to commit himself to left-wing causes such as the Black Panthers and the Palestine Liberation Organization. He further asserted his marginality by leaving Paris to live in Morocco and in Greece.

So determinedly outcast a career could not but exert an immense fascination—on philosophers such as Sartre and Derrida, but also on film-makers (Fassbinder's final film, *Querelle* (1982), is an adaptation of the novel *Querelle de Brest*) and musicians (David Bowie's song 'Jean Genie', whose hero 'lives on his back', is a homage to Genet). The marginality, the same-sex attraction, the dysfunctional or non-existent relationship with parents were obvious factors in Genet's fascination with the Papin case. *Les Bonnes* makes no explicit allusion to the Papins, and diverges markedly from the facts of their case—much as Genet's various accounts of his own life may well diverge from the (now unknowable) truth, or truths, about it. Derrida, in one of the most celebrated footnotes in the history of writing, articulates the need to go beyond the simplistic notion of biographical reference towards '[l]e nouveau statut—à trouver . . . celui des rapports entre l'existence et le texte, entre ces deux formes de textualité et l'écriture générale dans le jeu de laquelle elles s'articulent'[23] (Derrida 1967: 272). Of few writers is that more flamboyantly true than of Genet, and the remark can be applied with equal force to the Papin case and his treatment of it. Nicole Ward Jouve contends

---

[23] 'The new status—which is still to be identified—of the relationships between the life and the text, between these two forms of textuality and the general writing in whose play they are articulated.'

that he engages more closely than any other male writer with the gender aspects of the case, an engagement which is rendered possible by the intense stylization and strenuous non-realism of the play. This has only three characters, all female, but Genet wanted them to be played by men (which has seldom happened), largely in order to reinforce that stylization and the distanciation it brings about. There is doubtless a whiff of vaginaphobia about his injunction 'Les actrices sont donc priées, comme disent les Grecs, de ne pas poser leur con sur la table'[24] (Genet 1976: 8), but there is also an insistence on the separation between the biological body of the actor and the textual body s/he represents. That separation figures the separation between the biological and biographical bodies of the Papins and their victims on the one hand and the body of texts (including this one) to which they have given rise on the other, illustrating once more how far any treatment of the case is of necessity interpretative and textual.

Genet's maids bear the names Claire and Solange, while their mistress is simply Madame and Geneviève is absent. Claire 'is' Christine, the dominant partner, and Solange 'is' Léa, but simple equivalence of roles is rarely possible in Genet, and the process of identification is complicated here by the fact that the maids act out a ceremony in which Claire takes the part of Madame and Solange that of Claire. The ceremony is under way when the curtain rises. Claire/Madame begins by complaining about the 'éternels gants' ('eternal gloves') Solange/Claire leaves lying around—gloves that for Derrida in *Glas* signify the play's studied artifice and gender ambiguities. Claire plays a haughty Madame and Solange a by turns humble and domineering Claire, to whom the 'real' Claire/Madame attributes a lover, Mario ('Ce jeune laitier ridicule',[25] Genet 1976: 18), and even conceivably a child—both of course without any counterpart in Léa's life. Monsieur, far from being a respectable lawyer, is under arrest for theft and fraud, and Claire/Madame fantasizes that she will accompany him if need be to the penal colony in Guyana.

Already in this opening section we can see at work similar mechanisms of identification, usurpation, mirroring, splitting, and projection to those which have appeared, in less textually and linguistically complex form, in the Papin case and the psychoanalytic commentaries upon it. To quote Ian Magedera:

[24] 'The actresses are thus asked, as the Greeks have it, not to put their cunts on the table.'
[25] 'That ridiculous young milkman.'

In the intense and complex emotional atmosphere of the family, which includes hatred, jealousy and love, familial relations of power between the parent and child are played out in a sibling rivalry between Claire and Solange. They are also frequently reversed and overlaid by sexuality (one maid will dominate the other, only to be dominated herself in turn). (Magedera 1998: 5)

The echoes—the reflections—of Christine and Léa here are plain, yet Genet's introduction to the play, 'Comment jouer *Les Bonnes*', is at pains to rebut any suggestion that it is about 'real' maids or events ('Une chose doit être écrite: il ne s'agit pas d'un plaidoyer sur le sort des domestiques',[26] Genet 1976: 11). We shall be concerned here not only with tracing factual similarities and differences between the historical case and the literary text but, more importantly, with identifying themes, images, and tropes common to the two.

Claire/Madame speaks contemptuously of the maids' attic room, described as an 'infecte soupente'[27] (Genet 1976: 22), before declaring: 'Tu sens approcher l'instant où tu ne seras plus la bonne. Tu vas te venger'—an utterance which, taken with the anxious query: 'Tu aiguises tes ongles?'[28] (Genet 1976: 26), irresistibly reminds us of the Papin case. Yet it also looks away from that case, towards itself and the hermetic self-reflexive ritual of which it is a part, as is suggested by Claire/Madame's next line: 'Par moi, par moi seule, la bonne existe. Par mes cris et par mes gestes'[29] (Genet 1976: 27). Here Genet is clearly foregrounding the hieratic theatricality of his own play, in a move typical of his work. It is the tension between self-reflexivity and off-stage referent that imparts to *Les Bonnes* much of its characteristic ambiguity—a tension that there is not space to explore in our necessarily partial perspective here, but one nevertheless important to an appreciation of the text.[30] The conflation of the relationship between the two maids and that between maid and mistress, made possible by Claire and Solange's role-playing, offers suggestive parallels with the Papin case. Genet reworks that case in a manner strikingly similar to the Freudian dream-work, which relies upon on the one hand condensation—the merging of different signifieds under one signifier—and on the other

---

[26] 'One thing has to be written: this is not a plea about the fate of domestic servants.'
[27] (A) 'vile cupboard.'
[28] 'You can feel the moment coming when you won't be a maid any more. You're going to take your revenge . . . Are you sharpening your nails?'
[29] 'The maid exists by me and through me alone. Through my cries and my gestures.'
[30] Ian Magedera's monograph on the play (Magedera, 1998) deals quite comprehensively with this theme.

displacement—the diffusion of a signified across the signifying chain.[31] Thus, when Solange/Claire says to Claire/Madame: 'Je vous hais! Je hais votre poitrine pleine de souffles embaumés. Votre poitrine . . . d'ivoire! Vos cuisses . . . d'or! Vos pieds . . . d'ambre!'[32] (Genet 1976: 28), the amalgam of sensual intimacy and loathing of material superiority seems to combine or condense the love between the two sisters and their resentment of their employers. It also, and at the same time, displaces the opulence of the employer on to the loved/hated sister, in a twofold movement fundamental to the whole play and distilled in the 'real' Claire's whispering shortly afterwards 'Claire, Solange, Claire' (Genet 1976: 29).

When the alarm-clock rings the maids know that Madame will soon be back, and their game-playing for the time being comes to a stop. They discuss their performances almost in the manner of critics discussing a play, and we learn that Madame's lover Monsieur is under arrest because Claire has maliciously denounced him to the police and that Solange has tried to strangle Madame in her sleep. This more naturalistic section paradoxically takes us further away from the historical case, for it introduces a level of distanciation and detachment of which Christine and Léa were evidently incapable. Monsieur then telephones to say that he has been freed on bail. He is never to appear on stage, foreclosed like M. Lancelin from the drama of which he is an unwitting component, but his intervention is to prove decisive. The maids panic and decide to poison their mistress—a method of killing whose insidiousness puts it at the antipodes of that adopted by the Papins. Madame enters, complaining about the odious gladioli the sisters have bought in tones that for Derrida form part of the 'structure du gant, de la glace et de la fleur'[33] (Derrida 1974: 57) whose complex and sexually charged interplay suffuses the maids' ceremony.

Madame berates the sisters for their inappropriate attitude—decking the flat with flowers 'pour fêter juste le contraire d'une noce!'[34] (Genet 1976: 71)—but is exhilarated to discover that her loved one is now free, and bids Solange to summon a taxi with an extraordinary example of verbal and pronominal confusion ('dépêchez-toi'—Genet 1976: 82—'hurry up', the verb in the polite or formal form and the pronoun in the informal or familiar one) that mirrors the oscillations in the sisters'

---

[31] These concepts are articulated and developed in *The Interpretation of Dreams* (Freud, 1976: 381–419).

[32] 'I hate you! I hate your breast full of embalmed breaths. Your ivory breast! Your golden thighs! Your amber feet!'

[33] 'the structure of the glove, the mirror and the flower.'

[34] 'to celebrate the very opposite of a wedding.'

relationship to their mistress and each other. She declines to drink the poisoned lime tea prepared for her and goes to meet Monsieur, leaving the sisters' tumultuous and contorted feelings with no outlet but each other. In this respect the structure of Genet's play is the reverse—the mirror-image—of the Papin affair. The 'real-life' eruption of feelings long pent up *à deux* becomes the suicidal reflux of those feelings back into the incestuous couple, a reflux intensified by their resumption of the 'ceremony'. The sisters' linguistic and emotional union—like Siamese twins, to reprise Lacan—is concentrated in the interchange, apropos the announcement of Monsieur's release:

SOLANGE. La phrase a commencé sur ta bouche . . .
CLAIRE. Elle s'est achevée sur la tienne.[35]

(Genet 1976: 92)

The maids are horrified at Madame's discovery of their secret life together, including their reading of *Détective*, which as we have seen had dealt sympathetically with the Papin sisters, and the identities articulated by their 'ceremony' begin to fall apart. Claire can no longer distinguish clearly between Solange/Claire and Solange, and takes refuge in her identity as Madame, who denounces servants in ringing tones of class arrogance like that evoked by Le Guillant ('Les domestiques n'appartiennent pas à l'humanité',[36] Genet 1976: 100). Solange/Claire fantasizes in a long monologue her strangling of Claire/Madame and the death sentence that will inevitably follow ('Le bourreau me berce',[37] Genet 1976: 108). For Derrida that phrase is at the heart of *Les Bonnes* in its juxtaposition of apparent though similar-sounding opposites, the phallic executioner and the nurturing mother. That opposition, given their relationship with Clémence, had surely been more apparent than real for Christine and Léa.

Claire/Madame regains the upper hand at the last by commanding Solange/Claire to pour out the lime tea. Solange's terror at the prospect is perhaps appeased by Claire's reassurance, speaking as Claire: 'quand tu seras condamnée, n'oublie pas que tu me portes en toi'[38] (Genet 1976: 111). This yet again mirrors—if we remember that mirrors invert—the Papin case. Claire here articulates the 'need to return to her mother's womb' (Savona 1983: 66), which of course was the very reverse of Christine and Léa's killing of the symbolic mother. That reversal, however, is not the whole story, for the Papins' increased mutual absorp-

---

[35] 'The phrase started out in your mouth' . . . 'It ended in yours.'
[36] 'Servants are not part of humankind.'   [37] 'The executioner is cradling me.'
[38] 'when you are condemned, don't forget that you are carrying me within you.'

tion after the breach with Clémence showed how far they fulfilled the maternal role for each other, especially Christine for Léa. The physical, uterine nature of their intimacy is figured by the phrase 'tu me portes en toi', so that when Claire resumes her role as Madame and drinks the poisoned infusion it is as much a *Liebestod*, love issuing in death, as a gesture of despair or self-hatred.

No retelling of the plot of *Les Bonnes*, however basic, can fail to draw attention to the importance of mirrors and mirror-images in the play. At the beginning Claire is placed with her back to a dressing-table, as though refusing not just her own reflection (which she is in a sense doing by 'being' Madame) but the whole of that mirror-phase which had proved so complex and tormented for the Papin sisters. It is thus much more than a truism to say that Genet 'reflects' the Papin affair, even where he may appear to stray furthest from it. Claire's suicide following on a failed attempt to murder Madame plainly does not correspond to what happened in Le Mans in 1933, but if, as we have suggested earlier, Christine and Léa symbolically killed each other, and if Madame can in some sense be equated with 'maman', then Genet has effected a kind of secondary revision that brings him unnervingly close to the dynamic of the Papins' killings.

Philosophy lessons: Genet with Sartre and Derrida

Where Genet most obviously departs from the Papin case is in the baroque efflorescence of his maids' language. Early critics of the play took exception to this, André Ransan in the right-wing daily *L'Aurore* complaining: 'Les bonnes parlent comme des professeurs de philosophie et la patronne comme une chiffonnière'[39] (Magedera 1998: 41). Since Genet is notoriously anything but a realist playwright, this is a naïve criticism at best, but one which curiously suggests the kind of discourse to which the Papin case has, ever since Lacan, given rise. The two best-known works on Genet are Sartre's *Saint Genet, comédien et martyr* and Derrida's *Glas*—texts by probably the two best-known 'professeurs de philosophie' in post-war French history. Both in different ways are drawn to the artificiality of his writing and to the allocation and playing-out of roles within *Les Bonnes*. For Leo Bersani 'what interests

---

[39] 'The maids talk like philosophy teachers and their boss like a rag-and-bone lady.'

Genet is not how society distributes predicaments, but rather how it assigns identities' (Bersani 1995: 172)—though that might be thought to be an illusory opposition. The identities assigned by society to Christine and Léa surely turned out to be predicaments for them, and Claire's suicide at the end of the play just as surely suggests that there is no identity available for her that will shield her and her sister from the predicament in which they find themselves.

'La féminité sans femme: voilà ce que Genet veut nous présenter'[40] (Sartre 1952: 563). Christine and Léa, we have seen, were often regarded as 'women without femininity'—uninterested in male company or 'girlish' frivolities, so that even their array of finery was made by their own hands and destined solely for each other. Thus Sartre's remark, prescient in its foreshadowing of gender-based reading, might apply to the Papin sisters (to whom his analysis makes no direct allusion) as well as to Genet's maids:

> Ces fausses femmes qui sont de faux hommes, ces femmes-hommes qui sont des hommes-femmes, cette contestation perpétuelle de la masculinité par une féminité symbolique et de celle-ci par la féminité secrète qui fait la vérité de toute masculinité, tout cela ne constitue que le truquage de base. Sur ce fond évanescent paraissent des formes singulières: Solange et Claire.[41] (Sartre 1952: 565)

Solange and Claire for Sartre represent the Other of their mistress, loving her and thus wishing to become her, hating her and thus articulating Genet's hatred of a society that unceasingly sought to repress his own otherness. Sartre seems to us here closer to the subversive charge of *Les Bonnes* than Kate Millett, for whom the maids' 'favourite game is really not to play at murdering their mistress, but to play at being her. The second game is so much more exciting that they never get around to the first' (Millett 1977: 530). Millett's formulation minimizes if it does not ignore the fact that usurping somebody's identity can be a highly effective means of at least symbolically destroying that person, and in a Sartrean dialectical perspective also the social class and order of domination to which they belong.

That usurpation, however, is not confined to Claire's 'becoming' Madame; if it were, the play would be a much more straightforwardly

---

[40] 'Femininity without women—that is what Genet wants to present to us.'

[41] 'These false women who are false men, these women-men who are men-women, this perpetual challenging of masculinity by a symbolic femininity and of that in its turn by the secret femininity that is the truth of any masculinity—all this is merely the first stage of the play's trickery. Against this evanescent background there appear two strange shapes: Solange and Claire.'

committed one and its ending less imbued with tragedy. Solange's 'becoming' Claire complicates the relationship between the two sisters, of whom Sartre says: 'Elles se haïssent d'amour, comme tous les personnages de Genet'[42] (Sartre 1952: 567). This can of course also be said of the Papins, with whose complex bond the overlapping play of emotions and identities charted by Sartre has much in common. The 'pyramide de phantasmes' ('pyramid of fantasies') that is *Les Bonnes* negates a reality all too grimly manifested in the Papin killings and their aftermath, but, in keeping with the perverse dream-logic that is Genet's, negates it only to affirm it. Genet's desire is to 'ne jamais faire un *bon usage* de l'apparence'[43] (Sartre 1953: 573)—never to present that appearance as conforming to reality, never to endorse the bourgeois order of fixity and immutability against which in their different ways Genet and Sartre both wrote and acted, against which the Papin sisters can also be said, however unwittingly, to have directed their crime.

Jacques Derrida in *Glas* addresses the ways in which Genet's writing mounts a challenge to the unitary or bipolar identificatory norms of Western thought, among the most prominent of which are those of gender. The brief section on *Les Bonnes* thus concerns itself with such images as those of the gladiolus, the glove, and the mirror, rather than with the broader conceptual sweep that informs Sartre's analysis. For Derrida 'la cérémonie se maintient donc entre deux paires de gants se retournant sans cesse devant une glace'[44] (Derrida 1974: 58)—the inverted glove at once phallic and a clear figure of genital femininity (Derrida speaks elsewhere of the 'invagination' of texts in a similar context). The doubling-up of that glove and its mirroring figured in the Genet text as they were in the narcissistic involution of the Papin sisters' love.

Yet this is not to say that for Derrida *Les Bonnes* is 'about' anything so simple as same-sex incestuous love. The 'bourreau berceur', as we have seen a key image for him, condenses the conventional polarity of gender into a single androgynous figure, but a figure who does not appear on stage, who is:

> ... seulement représenté par chaque terme du trio identificatoire et spectaculaire. Qu'on ne doit pas se hâter de définir comme homosexuel: le quart exclu, décompté, décapité, toujours invisible mais jamais absent, toujours absent mais jamais sans effet, représenté par le gland tombé de l'arbre, les

---

[42] 'They hate each other with love, like all Genet's characters.'

[43] 'never to make a *good use* of appearance.'

[44] 'the ceremony therefore holds its ground between two pairs of gloves endlessly turning themselves/each other inside out in front of a mirror.'

gants, les glaïeuls ou les crachats, le bourreau coupé de la scène, le Monsieur ou le laitier (homologues phalliques) n'apparaissant au sein de ce qu'ils semblent mettre en mouvement que sous la non-espèce d'une écriture, et quasi anonyme, sans signature.[45]

This complex passage makes several allusions to imagery from *Les Bonnes* and to concepts deployed elsewhere in Derrida's work—notably that of signature—with which there is not space to deal here. What is essential for our purposes is the male as signifying absence—an absence/presence we have already seen figured in Nicole Ward Jouve's argument that 'the lack of a father figure of any kind is what made the situation ultimately murderous' (Ward Jouve 1998: 80). The unsigned writing to which Derrida alludes is, in the play, the anonymous letter denouncing Monsieur. If anything corresponds to this in the Papin case, it is the three letters written from prison by Christine after her crisis of July 1933, all addressed to male figures of authority ('homologues phalliques'), in which she moves from requesting a reunion with Léa to a humble acceptance of her punishment and desire to atone. Signed these letters undoubtedly are, but they are also denunciations—of Christine herself, filled with remorse for her deed and the lies she supposedly told about it under interrogation. The letters also, like that written by Claire and Solange in the play, prefigured (though they did not actually cause) their writer's death, for Christine's eventually fatal self-neglect in hospital was surely the only answer she could give to the question asked in one of them ('comment faire pour réparée [*sic*]',[46] Dupré 1984: 174).

Derrida, we should remember, is unlike Lacan or Dupré writing about the Genet play, not the Papin affair, of which he like Sartre makes no mention. Yet the importance of the excluded or foreclosed male, like that of mirroring and invagination, is strikingly similar in *Les Bonnes* and in its historical pre-text, so that Derrida's words—the very reverse or 'mirror-writing' of the 'écriture . . . quasi-anonyme, sans signature' he evokes—can be read as pertinent to both. Thus it is that, while Genet (like in their different ways Sartre and Derrida after him) diverges markedly from the historically attested facts, his text, and theirs, remain

---

[45] '. . . only represented by each term of the identificatory, specular trio. We should not be in too much of a hurry to describe this trio as homosexual, for the excluded fourth party, left out of account, decapitated, is always invisible but never absent, always absent but never without effect, represented by the acorn fallen from the tree, the gloves, the gladioli, or the spittle, the executioner cut out of the scene, the Monsieur or the milkman (phallic equivalents) who appear at the heart of the process they seem to set going only in the non-form of writing—a quasi-anonymous piece of writing, without a signature.'

[46] 'what can I do to make amends.'

true to the complex and bizarre unconscious logic that underlay the
Papin case, and has preoccupied writers on it ever since.

Wendy Kesselman's *My Sister in this House*

In 1982 Wendy Kesselman provided the second theatrical version of the
Papin affair after Genet's *Les Bonnes*. She was inspired to write the play
after reading Janet Flanner's texts on the Papin sisters and after visiting
Le Mans where she found the house still inhabited by Monsieur Lancelin.
She was struck particularly by the brown walls of the maids' room and
by the staircase which becomes, as Kilkelly points out, the structural
heart of the play. Kilkelly tells us: 'Comparing her own text to Genet's,
[Kesselman] comments that Genet's play could have happened any-
where. Her sense of the event is integrally tied to place; her play sees the
maids as victims of the house—hence the title *My Sister in this House*'
(Kilkelly 1986: 30). Kesselman's play also differs from Genet's in that she
removes Madame's lover and adds instead Madame's daughter, Isabelle,
because 'she felt strongly that it was to be a play about these four women,
the interweaving lives of these four women' (Hart 1989: 132). Men are
only present in the form of the voice-overs of the photographer, the
medical examiner, and the judge. Their role is simply to highlight various
aspects of the sisters' relationship and their relationship to their
employers. They are not rounded characters in their own right.

My Sister in this House consists of one act of sixteen scenes and is
performed without an intermission. This ensures that the build-up of
tension is not broken until the climax. The play opens with the voice-
over of Christine singing the lullaby 'Sleep my little sister, sleep' and the
light comes up slowly on Christine and Lea who are framed as if in a
photograph. The action therefore refers, as do so many of the texts which
consider the Papin affair, to the well-known photographs of the sisters.
There are three photographic incidents in all in the play: at the beginning, just past the middle of the play in scene 9, and at the end. Together
these constitute a metatext of the development of the sisters' story.
The first example is equivalent to the 'before' picture, the second time is
when they actually visit the photographer and this fills the gap between
'before' and 'after', and at the end of the play they stare out at the audience and stand 'as if framed in a photograph'—this obviously constitutes
the 'after' picture. The opening scene establishes the relationship
between the sisters, as much through what they are wearing as through
what they do. The difference in their ages is made clear by the way they

wear their hair. Christine's is worn in buns on each side of her head or in a braid circling her head, whilst Lea's hangs down in a braid. She is clearly still an adolescent. We are in a different household from that of the Danzards (the fictional name given to the Lancelins). Lea is is just starting out as a maid and Christine, her older sister, is giving her advice, thus establishing the relationship between the sisters as a mother–daughter relationship. The next time they are photographed by the photographer they are dressed identically in dark dresses with white lace collars and their hair is arranged in exactly the same way. When the photographer says that they look like twins or certainly sisters, Christine is at pains to establish the fact that she is older, but what we see belies what she says. At the same time the relationship between the sisters is blossoming into an incestuous one, although it does not fully flourish until scene 14. The final image of the play, which remains with the audience, is what they have become once the murders have taken place. Whereas the first scene begins with Christine singing to her younger sister, the last scene ends with Lea comforting her older sister with the lullaby. Christine's sleep will be that imposed by the guillotine to which she has been sentenced (the play does not say that her sentence is commuted).

My Sister in this House may be read as a 'going beyond' in terms of class, sexuality, and gender in that, as a piece of feminist theatre, it subverts the patriarchal and heterosexual economy by shifting the parameters of both femaleness and femininity. The ways in which it does this can be seen in three main areas: class is challenged through the use of clothing, heterosexuality through the incestuous lesbian relationship which develops between the maids, and gender through the fact that women, defined as 'passive' and 'non-violent' in patriarchal terms, take action and kill. What follows will look at each of these areas in turn through the dynamics of the relationships between the four women.

Early on in the play class boundaries are clearly defined. In scene 4 the maids have just served the Danzards their midday meal and have retreated to the kitchen. By means of simultaneous staging, we witness the conversation that takes place between mother and daughter and that between the two sisters. What the mistresses say is echoed by the sisters. Mirror images such as this are characteristic of the play in general (see, for example, Hart 1989). Madame remarks to Isabelle: 'They're so discreet. Not the slightest prying.' This is echoed by Christine saying to Lea: ' How lucky we are, Lea. The other houses I've been—they come into the kitchen and interfere. Madame knows her place.' Both Madame and Christine therefore appreciate that the other knows her place in terms of class and in terms of the power structures. If Madame Danzard is like Christine, Isabelle is like Lea, for their conversation also mirrors that of the other. Lea talking of Madame says: 'She doesn't let us get away with a thing.' This is echoed by Isabelle who remarks: 'Well Maman, let's face it—you don't let them get away with a thing', to which Madame replies: 'Why should I? I pay them enough', which, in turn, is echoed by Christine's 'Why should she? She wants the house a certain way'. This therefore establishes the pact that exists between the two pairs of women. The one is there to serve, the other is there to be served and both are content with this set-up. What is also established here is that the pact is unspoken. Dialogue only takes place between Madame Danzard and her daughter and between Christine and her sister, never between the two opposing pairs—that is, not until the penultimate scene of the play. Not speaking across the classes therefore emerges as a means of keeping class boundaries in place.

Problems arise between the two couples when the maids begin to step outside of their class and aspire to the position occupied by their mistresses. This is initially seen in the garments that they wear. In scene 7, Madame Danzard gives Isabelle a hat insisting that she wears it in order to impress their well-to-do friends. Immediately following this, and in the maids' room, Lea opens the trunk which contains beautiful lingerie and nightgowns sewn by Christine. These are garments which clearly belong, not to members of the working class, but to those of the middle class. The maids are transgressing the boundaries of class here by stepping outside of the one to which they are supposed to belong: Christine in buying such material and Lea in sporting the garments which Christine has made. This scene, which sees them overstep the boundaries of class, also sees them begin to transgress accepted sexual categories. Lea's trying on of the gown is essentially seductive and the scene ends with Christine admitting that her sister is beautiful.

The next time that they transgress the boundaries of class is in the visit to the photographer in scene 9. This takes place immediately after Madame has given Isabelle a photograph of them both together as a present. That the maids' visit to the photographer constitutes a transgression is made evident by the fact that they are both clearly frightened, a fear which Lea voices and which Christine tries to allay. The point is also made that the visit is expensive and once again it is clear that the maids are breaking out of the class to which they are supposed to belong by spending money which they are not supposed to have in the first place. Christine even refuses to take the photographer's offer of letting them have the photograph for half-price and renounces her working-class position by insisting on paying the full 50 francs.

Until now, however, the maids overstep the class boundaries only in their own room or outside of the house (at the photographer's), but soon they begin to stray beyond their class by taking their finer garments into other areas of the house. In scene 10 Lea comes downstairs in a pale pink sweater. That she has gone beyond her rights and broken the unspoken contract between the two pairs of women is stressed by Madame Danzard's reaction. She says to her daughter in Lea's hearing: 'What in heaven's name allows her to think she can wear a sweater like that in this house?' And later when Lea has gone to the kitchen she remarks: 'And how did she have the nerve, the extreme nerve to buy such a thing?' In a sense, Lea's wearing of the sweater here constitutes a form of revolt: she has dared to wear clothing more suited to the bourgeoisie in her mistresses' space. Again transgression in terms of class is echoed by transgression in terms of sexuality. Christine interprets the fact that Lea is wearing the sweater as an attempt to attract Isabelle and is jealous. Lesbian sexuality, this time across the class divide, is therefore brought to the fore. Isabelle, in turn, recognizes Christine's possessiveness and taunts her by seductively offering Lea a brush which she takes and with which she begins brushing Isabelle's hair. However, there is a sense in which class boundaries are maintained in that no word is exchanged in the interaction between Isabelle and Lea.

The maids now become bolder in wearing garments not belonging to their class. In scene 14 they return to the house one Sunday morning as Madame and Isabelle are about to go out. Christine and Lea are wearing identical coats and white gloves prompting Madame Danzard to remark: 'They don't even look like maids anymore.' Again this overstepping of class boundaries is linked to their sexual relationship at which Madame's remarks hint (Coffman 1999).

The donning of garments which do not rightfully belong to their class is mirrored by a parallel spoiling of garments which belong to the bourgeoisie. This firstly occurs when Christine alters Isabelle's dress in scene 13. Once again sexual tension is bound up with clothes. On noticing that Lea is smiling at Isabelle, Christine spoils the hem on the dress which is observed by Madame who complains to Isabelle but not directly to Christine. She then complains about the neckline which Christine begins to cut until Madame stops her and starts doing it herself. By now, of course, the dress is ruined. The next occasion is in scene 15 when the iron blows the fuse whilst Lea is ironing Madame's blouse which is then spoilt. This is also what finally blows the fuse in the relationship between the two pairs of women so to speak. Having burnt the garment, Christine and Lea go to their room to await the return of Madame. When the Danzards return to find that the maids are nowhere to be seen, Madame decides to go up the stairs to their room to find them. This is the first time that she has left the stage space belonging to her class and begins to venture into that of the maids. She sees that lights above are off and begins to go down the stairs again when Christine appears.

It is only now in this penultimate scene that Madame and Christine finally address each other. By leaving her own space and by addressing her maid directly, Madame Danzard is leaving the safety of her own class. She crosses the boundaries into the space of the working class and her language deteriorates accordingly, until she is threatening and insulting the sisters. What started out as an admonition for spoiling bourgeois property in the shape of the blouse ends up as a criticism of the sexual relationship which exists between the sisters. Although she does not name the nature of their relationship explicitly, she nevertheless insults them for being and doing that which is not named. Repression, which is a necessary corollary of being a female member of the dominant heterosexual class, finally gives way, resulting in the filthy tirade which issues from Madame's mouth. The implication is that this has been lurking beneath the well-to-do exterior all the time. Once Madame has insulted them and said that they will never work together again, both Christine and Lea act as one and fly at Madame and Isabelle. Violence is clearly present on both sides: in the one instance it is verbal and in the other it is physical. Class and gender barriers break down completely. In killing their mistresses, Christine and Lea do what women do not do: they resort to violence and they murder, not in a passive way but by ripping out eyes and smashing in skulls.

Faction, love, and the *polar*: Paulette Houdyer and Robert Le Texier

One of the two other works to be considered in this chapter is cast in the mould of the nineteenth-century realist or regional novel, the other, published in the Fleuve Noir series, in that of the *polar* or crime story. Both raise important questions to do with the affair, most notably around the writing (or non-writing) of its homoerotic components. Paulette Houdyer—the author of five other novels—is as we have already seen passionately attached to her native city and province, whose other major criminal scandal she deals with in the historical reconstruction *L'Affaire Caillaux*. This recounts the shooting of Gaston Calmette, the editor of *Le Figaro*, in 1914 by the wife of Joseph Caillaux, the former Finance Minister and a native of Le Mans, on whom Calmette was reported to hold compromising personal documents. Houdyer's book on the Papin sisters originally appeared as *Le Diable dans la peau* with the Parisian publishing house René Julliard in 1966, and was reissued under the title *L'Affaire Papin* by the small Le Mans press Cénomane in 1988. The preface, by the psychiatrist and psychoanalyst Martine Fleury, praises the 'intuition féminine' by which Houdyer was able to win Léa's confidence through telling her: 'Je sais que c'est une histoire d'amour'[47] (Houdyer 1988: 8). This is the major respect in which *L'Affaire Papin* differs from earlier treatments of the affair, which view it less as text than as pre-text, as raw material for poetic invention or pathological analysis. Fleury's preface at the same time alludes to the mirroring at work in the case ('Miroir des mots, miroir des êtres, miroir déplacé des passions des unes sur les autres'[48], Houdyer 1988: 7)—common ground with those earlier treatments in which it is omnipresent.

Houdyer's writing, as befits the genre within which she is working, is much more demotic than that of a Lacan or a Genet, creating atmosphere through the amassing of imagined or reconstructed conversations and local or period detail. The following quotation gives a good idea of her style:

> **Le vieux Mans méritait sa réputation de coupe-gorge. Peuplé le jour d'une marmaille au nez sale, de maritornes avachies s'injuriant autour des pompes et de touristes en troupes insolents, il s'éveillait la nuit à une vie moins bénigne et bruyante. A la lueur jaunasse des becs de gaz, les comptes se réglaient au couteau; dans la rue en escalier des Pans-de-Gorron, où prospéraient les lupanars, les imprudents étaient attaqués à la matraque en caoutchouc bourré de sable.[49] (Houdyer 1988: 14)**

We are here in the world of what Jill Forbes has called, referring to Carné's *Les Enfants du paradis*, 'a commonplace of popular literature, the thieves' kitchen or *cour des miracles* found in *The Beggar's Opera*, in Victor Hugo's *Notre-Dame de Paris*, and in a series of Expressionist films such as Pabst's *Threepenny Opera* (after Brecht)' (Forbes 1997: 25). That world survived into the early twentieth century (the Carné film, made under the Occupation, is of course set in the 1830s) in the popular fiction of such as Pierre MacOrlan and Francis Carco, with its respective evocations of Montmartre and Les Halles. Houdyer gives us an even more recent, and historically attested, manifestation of it in the centre of what

---

[47] 'I know that this is a love story.'

[48] 'A mirror of words, a mirror of beings, a displaced mirroring of the passions of some onto others.'

[49] 'The old part of Le Mans had a well-deserved reputation as a thieves' kitchen. Inhabited in the daytime by dirty-nosed brats, seedy sluts exchanging insults around the standpipes, and insolent flocks of tourists, its night life was less benign and rowdy. In the sallow light of the gas-lamps, accounts were settled with knives; on the steps that formed the rue des Pans-de-Gorron, where brothels thrived, the unwary would be attacked with rubber coshes filled with sand.'

was then a fairly small regional capital, lending *L'Affaire Papin* the sense of provincial exoticism that is to be one of its trademarks.

The discovery of the bodies is evoked in the historic present, a time-honoured device for the creation of suspense, and the first thing that the policeman Dézalée sees, provoking the remarkably restrained exclamation 'Nom de D . . . !', is 'un oeil humain', which 'n'exprime rien. Rien que l'ultime relâchement de la mort'[50] (Houdyer 1988: 22). Houdyer is the first writer on the case to give M. Lancelin so much as a walk-on part—a speaking one indeed, and one that places him in an explicitly Balzacian tradition, for when he learns that his wife and daughter are dead he cries out: 'Je veux les voir! . . . Elles sont à moi! . . . Je veux les voir. . . .'[51] (Houdyer 1988: 24). This is an unmistakable echo of Goriot's terrifying deathbed cry for his ungrateful daughters: 'Je veux mes filles! je les ai faites! elles sont à moi!'[52] (Balzac 1971: 344), and of the links between paternity and property at work throughout the *Comédie humaine*. The itemization of objects in the description of the house ('la table à repasser encore encombrée de la jeannette et du bol à humecter le linge, la chemise d'homme au col fripé qui la chevauche et le fer électrique posé sur sa semelle, à côté du porte-fer d'amiante',[53] Houdyer 1988: 26) likewise places Houdyer's writing in a realist tradition not hitherto encountered in writings on, or inspired by, the case.

The intensity of the revelation that Christine and Léa were lovers is all the greater for being situated in that tradition—for being proffered from within a mode of writing (what Barthes calls an *écriture*) for which to reprise the opening of *Le Père Goriot*, '*All is true*' (Balzac 1971: 22). There may be a suspicion of voyeurism, or its olfactory equivalent, about the description of the sisters' 'odeur exaltée par l'émotion: odeur de féminité maladive et de sueur âcre'[54] (Houdyer 1988: 30) when they are found in their room, though this might charitably be ascribed to their all-male 'audience'—four policemen—at the time. Léa's defiant 'Je suis sourde et muette!', referred to in Chapter 2, closes what in cinematic terms might be called the book's opening sequence, whereupon '[l]e "mystère" des filles Papin commence'[55] (Houdyer 1988: 31).

This leads into the 'flashback' recounting of the sisters' lives that takes up the bulk of Houdyer's text. The facts she retails have by and large been

---

[50] 'a human eye . . . expressing nothing but the final loosening of death.'
[51] 'I want to see them! They're mine! I want to see them!'
[52] 'I want my daughters! I made them! They're mine!'
[53] 'the ironing-table with its sleeve and the bowl for moistening the clothes, the man's shirt with its frayed collar lying across it, and the electric iron next to its asbestos holder.'
[54] 'a smell intensified by emotion—a smell of sickly femininity and bitter sweat.'
[55] 'The "mystery" of the Papin girls begins.'

dealt with in Chapter 2 of our study. What is worthy of more attention is the perspective in which she deals with them. Nicole Ward Jouve singles out her account for its unusual empathy with the sisters, an empathy largely grounded in the material and affective poverty of their early lives. The main street of Marigné, their native village, is described in anything but Arcadian terms:

> Deux rangées de maisons basses, accolées à la diable et comme mortes, toute vie drainée par des ruelles nourries d'ombre vers la campagne sarthoise, ses terres à blé, ses vignes, ses vaches rouquines au pis desquelles parfois, aux heures chaudes, une vipère vient boire.[56] (Houdyer 1988: 34)

This is the world of Zola's *La Terre* (set in the adjacent province of Beauce) or even, as the adder may suggest, Hardy's *The Return of the Native*—a rural dystopia characterized by the thirteen pregnancies that brought the Papins' grandmother to the brink of suicide and the exhausting hours Gustave was to work to support his wife and children. Isabelle, the sisters' 'spinster aunt' by whom they were initially brought up, appears in this context less as a sinister influence than as a proto-feminist role-model, who 'à petites doses quotidiennes, patientes' would impart to Christine 'sa méfiance des mâles'[57] (Houdyer 1988: 41). If she comes close to seeming the heroine of this early part of the narration, this is largely in opposition to Clémence, portrayed in bold primary colours as its villainess. Having sexual relations with Gustave 'de temps en temps, pour le récompenser, comme on donne un morceau de sucre à un chien'[58] (Houdyer 1988: 46), while squandering his earnings and supposedly cheating on him to satisfy 'ses appétits de femme jeune et jolie'[59] (Houdyer 1988: 59), she is constructed as a more ruthless and less tragic version of Flaubert's Emma Bovary. This seems to act as sufficient justification for Gustave's seduction of Emilia, described in terms reminiscent of soft-core pornography rather than of Nabokov's *Lolita* ('une maîtresse de onze ans à la beauté précoce, à la croupe ronde et aux petits seins durs',[60] Houdyer 1988: 72). Nicole Ward Jouve is not the only one to find this disconcerting ('it is hard to swallow the idea that ten- or eleven-year-old Emilia was so happy to be seduced by her father', Ward Jouve 1998: 76).

---

[56] 'Two rows of low houses, flung together any old how and all but dead, any life drained out of them by the shadowy lanes leading to the Sarthe countryside, its cornfields and vines, its russet cows at whose udder sometimes when it is hot an adder will come and drink.'

[57] 'in tiny, patient daily doses . . . her mistrust of males.'

[58] 'now and then, to reward him, as one gives a dog a sugar-lump.'

[59] 'the appetites of an attractive young woman.'

[60] 'a precociously beautiful eleven-year-old mistress, with an already plump behind and small but firm breasts.'

The breach with Gustave and removal to Le Mans, away from this world of abusive sexuality and back-breaking toil, might have appeared a welcome escape for Christine and Léa; but the rigours of the Bon Pasteur with its monthly partially clothed baths were fully a match for those of life in Marigné. Houdyer describes Christine's fascination with the embroidered vestments in the chapel sacristy, in terms that recall Genet's ritualistic obsessions:

> **Les couleurs émergeaient de l'obscurité, lentement. Sauf certain blanc de pâte de menthe immuable et plat, les blancs se réchauffaient, crémeux. Les violets prenaient un éclat lapidaire et, de l'améthyste, viraient au grenat, verdissaient au passage le bleu du manteau qui habillait la Sainte Vierge, les jours de procession.[61] (Houdyer 1988: 84)**

The colour imparted by the trappings of Catholicism to the dreariness of provincial existence is a common theme in the realist novel, from Stendhal's *Le Rouge et le noir* on, and serves here to prepare us for Emilia's decision to go into a convent and Christine's temptation to do likewise. Clémence's ferocious response to Christine ('La gifle claqua, brutale, sèche',[62] Houdyer 1988: 92) casts her more firmly than ever as, biological ties notwithstanding, a variant of the wicked stepmother, who sometimes seems to be burdened with sole responsibility for what was to happen fifteen or so years later.

Léa was subjected according to Houdyer to constant sexual harassment from one of her employers and his friends ('Ils la tâtaient partout. "Regardez-moi ces cuisses-là! Et ce derrière de lapin écorché! . . . Les nénés lui poussent pourtant!"',[63] Houdyer 1988: 110). There is of course no way now of establishing whether or not these allegations are true—a problem more troublesome in dealing with Houdyer's densely detailed reconstruction of the affair than for any of the other texts under consideration. The most one can say is that, given the close relationship Houdyer was to develop with Léa and the degree of harassment to which serving-maids were often subject, there is every likelihood that they were justified, and that the bond between the girls may have derived much of its exclusive intensity from Christine's consequent protectiveness towards her younger sister ('. . . ça l'était: laid, sale . . . répugnant! Ces

---

[61] 'The colours slowly emerged from the darkness. Except for one flat and invariable peppermint-white, the whites became warmer and more creamy. The purples took on a jewel-like glitter and from amethyst turned to garnet, as they did so turning the blue of the Virgin Mary's processional cloak green.'

[62] 'The slap rang out, brutal and harsh.'

[63] 'They used to feel her all over. "Just look at those thighs! And that backside like a skinned rabbit! . . . Still, her tits are growing nicely".'

gestes-là n'étaient ni apitoyés, ni paternels, ils . . . Enfin, Léa ne devait pas les supporter, c'est tout!',[64] Houdyer 1988: 111).

It is shortly after this that we find the first explicitly erotic passage, Christine initiating Léa into '[l]'éblouissante vérité du plaisir' which she had herself discovered, literally, by chance ('Jaillie d'une caresse machinale, la délivrance l'a surprise',[65] Houdyer 1988: 133). Houdyer is the first writer to dwell on the sisters' reciprocal erotic pleasure, only hinted at by Lacan—something her gender may help to make less problematic. Because lesbian scenes are such a hardy perennial of erotic or pornographic texts designed primarily for heterosexual male consumption, it would have been very hard for a male to sign passages such as Houdyer gives us without at least a taint of prurience. She is able, on the other hand, to present their bodily closeness as one of the few sources of joy and warmth in an otherwise grim existence, one where for their employers ' "Bonnes," dans leur bouche, cela signifie: "Bonnes qu'à ça" '[66] (Houdyer 1988: 144). The writing in these episodes is not particularly explicit—by contemporary standards indeed positively discreet. Thus, in 'la volupté de se savoir complices, de respirer chacune l'odeur de l'autre sur sa propre peau, montant par l'entrebâillement de sa robe ou collée à ses doigts'[67] (Houdyer 1988: 186), only the 'collée à ses doigts' is likely to cause even the mildest raising of eyebrows. Geneviève—until the evening of the crime almost as absent from texts on it as M. Lancelin—finds her place too in this gynaeceum of desire, as 'le pôle d'attraction de la maison' for Léa in particular whose interest she encourages with the use 'de ses yeux gris, de ses longues mains, d'un rire exténué de colombe'[68](Houdyer 1988: 174). Her dove-like quality is presumably in part accounted for by the (hetero)sexual innocence that she shared with the Papin sisters, and her attractiveness for Léa is to be gruesomely reworked when her body is mutilated on the night of the crime.

Destiny becomes a key player when the sisters meet the psychic Beloeuf, who predicts that they will remain united until death and on a later visit utters words that strikingly predate those Christine was famously to pronounce in custody ('Dans une vie antérieure, votre soeur

---

[64] '. . . it was ugly, dirty, . . . repulsive! Those gestures were not well-meaning or paternal, they . . . Well, Léa should not stand for them, that was all!'

[65] 'The dazzling reality of pleasure . . . Springing from a mechanical caress, the release took her by surprise.'

[66] ' "Maids," for them, just means: "That's all they're good for." ' There is a pun here on the two senses of 'bonnes'—'maids' and 'good'.

[67] 'the voluptuous knowledge that they were accomplices, that each breathed the other one's smell on her own skin, through the opening of her dress or sticking to her fingers.'

[68] 'the centre of attraction in the household . . . with her grey eyes, her long hands, her worn-out dove-like laughter.'

et vous . . . Je le savais. Vous avez été mari et femme!',[69] Houdyer 1988: 184). This works to reinforce their 'lien nouveau, cette seconde fraternité de leurs sangs'[70] (Houdyer 1988: 185)—recounted by Houdyer as an unfolding love story, the discovery of 'le double qu'on cherche depuis la naissance, celui qui partage et comprend, dont la présence anime les beautés du monde et qui fait de la vie un chant'[71] (Houdyer 1988: 186). This is sentimental, but also in its way dramatic—a happy ending arriving prematurely, before the real tragic ending readers of the book will already know. The sisters' relative satisfaction with their employer goes hand in hand with a widening gulf between them and their mother, for whom Christine was to be known merely as 'l'aînée'/'the elder one'. The final meeting between mother and daughter, shortly after the town hall episode, is marked by Clémence's cursing Christine ('Je te maudis! . . . Tu ressembles à ton père! . . . Il était capable de tout . . . Il aurait dû mourir sur l'échafaud . . . Tu mourras . . .',[72] Houdyer 1988: 210)—in the dramatic perspective of the work a distillation and concretization of the emotional blight she had already inflicted.

That curse of course comes to fruition on the fateful evening, recounted almost entirely in dialogue. The tension is stoked through the accumulation of vocabulary pertaining to the eyes and to sight, reminding us perhaps that for Sartre and Lacan in their very (but not totally) different ways the look or gaze of the Other is a key factor in the construction, and possible unmaking, of subjectivity. The sisters' 'unnatural' relationship is now plain to see ('Votre tenue me m'aurait-elle pas ouvert les yeux que, maintenant, j'aurais compris!'); Mme Lancelin reproaches herself for her failure to see what was going on under her nose ('Ai-je été aveugle, hein? Ah, vous deviez penser que j'avais les yeux bouchés!',[73] Houdyer 1988: 225); and the murderous attack is triggered by her threat 'Je crierai bien haut ce que j'ai vu! De mes yeux vu!'[74] (Houdyer 1988: 226). We leave the murder scene with Léa fiercely mutilating the cadavers while Christine laughs wildly.

Little space is devoted to the trial—more a matter of record than the intimate aspects of the case that interest Houdyer—and we bid farewell

---

[69] 'In an earlier life, you and your sister . . . I knew it. You were husband and wife!'
[70] (their) 'new bond, that second sisterhood of their mingled blood.'
[71] 'the double we look for from the moment we are born, the one who shares and understands, whose presence brings the beauties of the world alive and turns life into a song.'
[72] 'I curse you! . . . You're like your father . . . He was capable of anything . . . He should have died on the scaffold! You'll die . . .'
[73] 'Even if your state of undress hadn't opened my eyes I'd have understood now! . . . Was I blind or what? Oh, you must have thought that my eyes were sealed!'
[74] 'I'll shout out loud what I've seen—seen with my own eyes!'

to the sisters in a one-page epilogue that tells of the 'dignité de mari bafoué' with which Christine severed all links with her sister and of Léa's quiet life since her release, in a city which Houdyer, unlike the *France-Soir* journalist in the same year, refrains from naming. 'Elle voulait qu'on l'oublie, elle y est parvenue'[75] (Houdyer 1988: 247)—an assertion piquantly undercut by the very book in which it is made. Paulette Houdyer has described her in conversation as a grey and ghostly figure, burnt out by the enormity of what she had been party to and still cleaving to the memory of the sister who had been the only human being to love her.

A certain critical aesthetic—one not foreign to the authors of this book—might be tempted to dismiss Houdyer's periodic luridness and her perhaps overemphatic evocations of provincial life. These may appear sensationalist—lacking in what the sociologist Pierre Bourdieu would refer to as 'distinction'[76]—compared to the other writings on the case we have examined; but is that any more than a way of saying that Houdyer draws attention to material, sensual, erotic aspects of the Papins' life which those other, more 'distinguished' texts ignore or embroider? It might also be to dismiss the passionate empathy she brings to the sisters (despite its title, *L'Affaire Papin* is about Christine and Léa much more than it is about a judicial affair or a psychoanalytic case), and thereby to forget that the constructedness of individuals so beloved of much critical theory does not rob those individuals' experiences of their affective value or lived reality. Christine and Léa live, troublingly, as characters in the classic realist sense through as well as in spite of *L'Affaire Papin*'s sometimes unsubtle treatment of them.

Robert Le Texier's *Les Soeurs Papin* is the most recent literary treatment of the case, dating from 1994. The publishing house Série noire, founded by Marcel Duhamel in 1945, was responsible for popularizing in France the American detective novels of such as Dashiell Hammett and Raymond Chandler, as well as for fostering French writers in the genre, notably Léo Malet. The post-war French enthusiasm for American popular culture, evidenced in the jazz cellars of Saint-Germain-des-Prés and the influence of Hollywood *film noir* on the New Wave directors, surfaced also in a proliferation of pulp fiction (*polar*) series, and later in the spawning of journals and clubs devoted to the genre. But Le Texier's book, despite the title of the series in which it appeared,

---

[75] 'the dignity of a snubbed husband . . . She wanted to be forgotten, she has succeeded.'
[76] See Bourdieu 1979 for development of this concept.

is much closer to the 'factional' reconstruction of Paulette Houdyer than to the *noir* genre. There is no detective hero (unless we cheat by counting Le Texier himself, on the trail of a motive or motives rather than of a criminal identity never for a moment in doubt), and little of the urban cynicism normally found in the *polar*, which would scarcely be appropriate in the sleepy Le Mans we may (re)recognize at the beginning of the novel ('Depuis le début de cet après-midi gris et froid de février 1933, la grande maison des Lancelin, au creux d'un quartier tranquille de la bonne ville du Mans, était silencieuse et paraissait désert',[77] Le Texier 1994: 11).

The major themes we have found in other accounts of the affair, particularly Houdyer's, are all present and correct, including the influence of class and region (Mme Lancelin is said to have mocked the patois expressions the sisters occasionally used), the importance of sight—the look, the gaze—in triggering the explosion (Mme Lancelin provokes this by asking Christine: 'Où est Léa? Je veux la voir!',[78] Le Texier 1994: 25), and the incestuous relationship, recounted in somewhat hackneyed 'softcore' terms as the sisters, perhaps following Marie Antoinette's advice, enjoy *brioche* in bed together:

> **Léa . . . , souffla-t-elle [sc. Christine].**
> **Ses doigts glissèrent sur le cou, les seins, le ventre. Léa avait fermé les yeux. La lueur vacillante de la bougie projetait sur son beau visage offert au plaisir des ombres fugitives . . .[79] (Le Texier 1994: 21)**

The two sisters on their discovery are described as looking very similar, except that '[s]eul le regard était différent'[80] (Le Texier 1994: 46). After part one's account of the killings, part two, as in Houdyer, reconstructs the sisters' earlier life, in a narration sprinkled with patois which, again like Houdyer, unproblematically casts Clémence as the villainess of the piece, callously rejecting not only her husband but her own children ('Ses gamines, elle n'en voulait pas, elle ne les avait jamais voulues, il le savait, c'était par force qu'elle s'était mariée avec lui, et elle avait eu tort',[81] Le Texier 1994: 67). A rather unsubtle textual strategy of Le Texier is to

---

[77] 'Since the beginning of this cold grey February afternoon in 1933, the Lancelins' big house, nestling in a quiet area of the good city of Le Mans, had been silent and appeared deserted.'

[78] 'Where is Léa? I want to see her!'

[79] 'Léa . . . , breathed Christine. Her fingers slid across her neck, her breasts, her belly. Léa had closed her eyes. The flickering light of the candle cast fleeting shadows across her beautiful face, given up to pleasure . . .'

[80] 'Only the look/gaze was different.'

[81] 'She didn't want her girls, she had never wanted to have them, he knew that, theirs had been a shotgun wedding and she had made a mistake.'

scatter his narration with premonitions of the already-related climax; thus, Clémence's threats to put Léa out to nurse are uttered 'les yeux exorbités'[82] (Le Texier 1994: 82)—the very phrase used earlier (Le Texier 1994: 42) to describe the reaction of one of the policemen on discovering the crime. Similarly, when the sisters are hurt in an accident with a horse and cart, 'le sang de leurs plaies s'était trouvé mêlé', leaving them 'liées par le sang!'[83] (Le Texier 1994: 91)—a foreshadowing at once of the threefold menstrual bleeding that was taking place on 2 February and of the ties of blood, familial and homicidal, that were to bind together the Papins and their victims.

Le Texier appears more perplexed than Houdyer by the sisters' lack of interest in the opposite sex, even though his somewhat moralistic condemnation of their mother's alleged series of 'admirers' and account of the lascivious attitude of males towards Léa when she first went into service would seem to provide at least some reason for it. He speaks of their 'absence étonnante de fréquentations masculines alors qu'elles étaient dans l'épanouissement des attraits de la jeunesse et ne présentaient aucune malformation physique de nature à faire fuir les éventuels prétendants'[84] (Le Texier 1994: 134–5). He accounts for the crime by 'un subit accès de folie furieuse'[85] (Le Texier 1994: 141)—a diagnosis as incontestable as it is unhelpful, though as we have seen one not accepted by the court and first formulated *in extenso* by Lacan.

The class dimension of the case is also evoked, but Le Texier does this in terms which suggest that unconsciously at least the text is gesturing towards more than that when it alludes to 'la haine envers un monde froidement dominateur, étranger à la douceur et à l'affection, un monde fermé, à jamais inaccessible, mais un monde admiré tout autant que redouté, et inconsciemment désiré'[86] (Le Texier 1994: 178). This is the master/servant world of Le Guillant, but it would also be quite a serviceable description of the sisters' tormented relationship with their mother—herself on Le Texier's account bereft of affection for them and forever out of reach, yet also unconsciously desired, as their referring to Mme Lancelin as 'maman' and Léa's subsequent return to a life with Clémence surely show. Léa's supposed wish, towards the end of her life,

---

[82] 'her eyes bulging out of her head.'
[83] 'the blood of their wounds had been intermingled . . . bound together by blood.'
[84] 'surprising absence of male company when they were in the full bloom of youth and had no physical malformation that might have frightened off potential suitors.'
[85] 'a sudden attack of furious madness.'
[86] 'hatred for a coldly dominating world, with no gentleness or affection, a world that was closed and forever out of reach, but one admired quite as much as it was feared, and unconsciously desired.'

to go back to Le Mans, join Emilia in her convent, and pray with her for Christine's soul (Le Texier 1994: 189) appears in this light more than the pious wish of a Flaubertian 'coeur simple'.[87] It was surely rather a desire to reconstruct the security and closeness she had only ever known in the implosive form of the couple she formed with her elder sister. Finally reconciled in life with her mother, in her imagination with Emilia, and in the safe, not to say necessary, distance of death with Christine, Léa's final wish would have given her a family unit dispersed across space and time, in which neither the absent/intrusive father nor the exploitative surrogate mother/employer found a place – a happy ending of a kind.

---

[87] The reference here is to Félicité, the simple-hearted and self-sacrificing servant heroine of Flaubert's short story *Un coeur simple*.

4 Cinematic Reproductions

This chapter will examine three cinematic interpretations of the Papin affair: Nico Papatakis's *Les Abysses* (1963), Nancy Meckler's *Sister my Sister* (1994), and Claude Chabrol's *La Cérémonie* (1995). (Reference to Denis's *Les Blessures assassines* and Ventura's *En quête des soeurs Papin* can be found in the Afterwor.) These films put the spectator in a privileged position, for he or she is able to witness an event which, apart from the participants, had no witnesses. The killings are explored in the films in two main ways: the one political, where property and ownership (to differing degrees and in differing ways) are at the heart of the conflict; the other psycho-sexual, where the focus is on the relationship between the sisters and between the sisters and their employers. It is indeed interesting to note that those made in France, *Les Abysses* and *La Cérémonie*, concentrate more heavily on the political and class aspects than the British production *Sister my Sister* which, for the most part, focuses its attention on the relationships between the women. This is not to say that class does not play an important role (it does as Coffman in her reading of *Sister my Sister* makes clear), just that it is not foregrounded in the same way. Such a statement may at first seem strange given that the class system is more explicit in a country which still has a monarchy than in a country which has been a Republic for over 200 years. However, we must remember that France is a nation which has undergone more than one revolution and has felt the effects of the revolt of its peasants, a nation which both champions the revolt of the workers (many of its greatest intellectuals also supported the communist cause) and fears it (as it is manifested in Zola's mob for instance). Because this reading will demonstrate how they are thematically similar, *La Cérémonie* will follow *Les Abysses*, despite the fact that it appeared a year after *Sister my Sister*.

Both *Les Abysses* and *La Cérémonie* highlight the ways in which the Papin killings act as a paradigm, in terms of the master/slave dialectic, for other examples of conflict in society. Papatakis's film was released in 1963, just after the end of the Algerian war in which the French colonizers were defeated and for which *Les Abysses* was seen as a metaphor. *La Cérémonie* appeared in the 1990s in a society in which many immigrants suffer, like Sophie, the heroine of *La Cérémonie*, because they are illiterate. Language and access to it, as our reading of Chabrol's film will demonstrate, is one of the instruments of political and cultural power; to have inadequate access to language means to be powerless. *La Cérémonie* was also released at the same time as other films which deal with class conflict in a France that on the surface might appear classless. For instance, Chabrol points to Kassovitz's *La Haine* (1995) which treats the problems of the 'banlieue' and of cultural minorities. He likens what happens in Kassovitz's film to an 'explosion' and what happens in his own to an 'implosion': both disrupt and undermine the status quo (Berthomieu, Jeancolas, and Vassé 1995: 9).

La Cérémonie also coincides with a spate of films, including *Sister my Sister*, which deal with women and violence and which follow in the wake of a general interest in this topic throughout the 1980s and 1990s in the domain of gender studies. Until then women and violence had been explained from a masculine, essentially biased and often misogynistic, point of view. This, of course, goes back to the work of the 'father' of modern criminology, the Italian scientist, Cesare Lombroso, whose *The Female Offender* (1893) posited, amongst other things, that women who commit violent crime have the physiognomy of men (Jones 1980: 4). Interpretations of the 'after' pictures of the Papin sisters, notwithstanding that of the Surrealists, indicate that this view is by no means the exception. That physiognomy determines criminality is still very much the case in mainstream popular cinema where the villain's face reflects his criminal nature. At the other extreme, if the villain is female, she is often the *femme fatale* endowed with phallic characteristics (through an overinvestment of body parts such as the breasts or legs or by wearing a slinky gown) and is thereby 'masculinized'. The portrayal of the Papin sisters in the texts by Meckler and Chabrol (and to a certain extent Papatakis), however, in which the women are young, attractive, and clearly feminine, does much to refute this idea and, in some ways, their very femininity makes the viciousness of the crime even more difficult to comprehend, such are our prejudices.

On the other hand, the Papin affair does at first sight seem to constitute a very female crime. Ann Jones asserts: 'Unlike men, who are apt to stab a total stranger in a drunken brawl or run amok with a high powered rifle, we women usually kill our intimates: we kill our children, our husbands, our lovers' (1980: pp. xv–xvi). The sisters kill women of whose daily existence they have been part for some considerable time and they do this within what has traditionally been women's space: the home. However, the way in which the murders are carried out questions more recent assumptions about how and why women kill. In their work *The Lust to Kill: A Feminist Investigation of Sexual Murder* (1987), Deborah Cameron and Elizabeth Frazer explore the category of the 'sex crime' which they see as belonging almost exclusively to the male preserve and which came into being in the late nineteenth century in the wake of discourses initially inspired by the Marquis de Sade. Exceptions to the male sex killer include the Countess Bathory who bathed in the blood of her eighty girl victims and more recently Myra Hindley, whom Cameron and Frazer go on to exclude from their list because she acted with and for Ian Brady. They state: 'Whereas rape, sexual assault, necrophilia, breast and genital mutilation are the common place of male sexual killing, these are for the most part practices quite alien to women. The "psychology of sexual criminals", which permits a Peter Sutcliffe to climax while stabbing, is evidently a type of masculine psychology: sexual murder is a distinctly male crime' (1987: 25).

The Papin murders, especially as they are interpreted in the films, clearly demonstrate that sex and violence are not the sole preserve of men. They combine what is essentially deemed a female crime—it is per-petrated within the domestic domain and against people who are inti-mates, almost part of the family (the sisters called Madame 'maman' in her absence)—with aspects of what Cameron and Frazer view as the male 'sex crime'—they pluck out their mistresses' eyes (eyes and testi-cles being analogous), bare the legs of the younger woman and mutilate her legs, buttocks, and genitals with a bread knife (which is unmistak-able phallic penetration). The Papin killings therefore fail to fall neatly into a prescribed category of crime according to sex and open the way to different explorations of the nature of violent crime in terms of gender, which the films exploit to the full.

It is also of consequence that new reproductions of the Papin case in the films by Meckler and Chabrol should appear in a decade which saw its first female (lesbian) serial killer in Aileen Worunos, the Florida prostitute who killed seven men. Unlike the Papin sisters she killed strangers and more than once, but like them she too had an intimate relationship with another woman who was like a sister to her. She inverted the dominator/dominated dichotomy and in so doing she dis-turbed the profile of the serial killer, not only because she was a woman and a prostitute—normally prime targets of serial killers—but also because her victims were from the dominant class. They were all middle-aged white males, whom she killed, she would have us believe, in self-defence. Michele Aaron also suggests that it is perhaps no coincidence that the release of films like *Sister my Sister* should coincide with the trial of Rosemary West who was part of a murderous couple, had lesbian relationships, and murdered both her own children and strangers (1999: 81).

Aaron also points to the fact that *Sister my Sister*, along with other films released at the same time such as *Heavenly Creatures* (Peter Jackson, 1994), *Fun* (Rafael Zelinsky, 1994), and *Butterfly Kiss* (Michael Winterbottom, 1995), constitute the new genre of 'lesbian couples who kill' which draws on elements of the female buddy movie and the erotic thriller (1999). Lesbianism is therefore seen to come into its own in these texts and attempts to move away from its status as an appropriated male fantasy at a time when society is beginning to give more credence to same-sex couples.

The Papin affair therefore constitutes a special case and this is made all the more explicit by the films which it has inspired. Not only does it act as a paradigm for various aspects of the master/slave dialectic which is still evident in contemporary society, but it also raises questions about women's relationships with each other and with sex and violence. This section will therefore differ from the preceding sections in that it will use the Papin affair, with whose facts and written reproductions the reader will by now be familiar, as the paradigm through which issues pertaining to the contemporary context such as class, culture, and gender are explored.

Nico Papatakis's *Les Abysses*

When it first appeared in 1963 *Les Abysses* caused a stir: the selection committee at Cannes refused it entry to the Film Festival of that year and this prompted five French literati to voice their support of the film in *Le Monde* in April 1963. André Malraux, the then Minister of Culture, also interceded on the film's behalf and insisted that it represent France in the Festival. At Cannes it provoked an outcry and the film remains controversial to this day. As late as 1998, it had still not been shown on French television (*Positif* 1998: 57). However, it is available on video cassette in the United States where one suspects that Wendy Kesselman's play *My Sister in this House* and later her screenplay for *Sister my Sister* had a large role to play in arousing interest in it. It was released in 1996 by Hollywood's Attic (a safe place to be sure to keep the mad women who figure in the film, when one bears in mind Gilbert and Gubar's seminal text *The Madwoman in the Attic*) and the spectator should bear in mind that the subtitles leave a lot to be desired.

Reviled by many, *Les Abysses* was nevertheless revered by the likes of Sartre, Beauvoir, Genet, Breton, and Prévert in the 1963 issue of *Le Monde* and it was even hailed by Simone de Beauvoir as one of the greatest films that she had ever seen. For Breton, who echoes what is said by Eluard and Péret in their piece on the Papin sisters, the maids, played by the real sisters Colette and Francine Bergé, 'sont belles comme la foudre';[1] and for Prévert, who cannot resist poetry in his prose, they are 'belles comme le jour et la nuit, folles, cruelles et tendres, comme l'est si souvent la vie'.[2] Such *romantic* appraisals recall at once Adolphe's description of Ellénore as 'un bel orage' (a 'beautiful storm') in Constant's *Adolphe*, and Byron's poem, 'She walks in beauty like the night'. With *Les Abysses*, says Breton, 'nous sondons l'éperdu des passions humaines'[3] and indeed it is easy to see why Papatakis called his film *Les Abysses*.

Comments in this edition of *Le Monde* also centre on the class conflict which is so evident in the film. Beauvoir reiterates here a statement first formulated in *La Force de l'âge*: 'Seule la violence du crime commis par les deux héroïnes nous fait mesurer l'atrocité du crime invisible dont elles ont été victimes',[4] and this is echoed by Sartre who considers that the sisters' victims become the real perpetrators of the crime: 'Mais peu à peu le retournement s'amorce: les inconsistantes victimes se découvrent commes les véritables bourreaux. A travers leur mollesse et leur insignifiance, ces trois bourgeois représentent l'ordre de fer qui a condamné les deux soeurs dès la naissance.'[5] Prévert sees both parties as essentially malevolent calling the sisters 'déesses infernales qui tourmentent les méchants'.[6] Since these somewhat cursory reviews, *Les Abysses* has not elicited much critical attention. After a general discussion, this section will go some way towards filling the gap by examining two main issues highlighted in the film: property rights and interpersonal relations.

Papatakis's original intention had been to make a film of *Les Bonnes*. However, when he pulled a publicity stunt by inviting the press to photograph Jeanne Moreau and Annie Girardot in maid's uniforms, he and Genet, who had been good friends at the time, argued and Genet withdrew the rights to the film (White 1993: 528). Papatakis then decided to refer back to the actual *fait divers* and turned to the playwright, Jean Vauthier, for his screenplay. An initial viewing of the film, however, does

---

[1] 'are beautiful like thunder.'

[2] 'beautiful like day and night, cruel and tender as life so often is.'

[3] 'we sound the depths of human passion.'

[4] 'Only the violence of the crime committed by the two heroines makes us appreciate the atrocity of the invisible crime of which they were victims.'

[5] 'But little by little a reversal occurs: the victims find that they are the real henchmen. Beneath their weakness and insignificance, these three bourgeois represent the iron order which condemned the two sisters from birth.'

[6] 'infernal goddesses who torment the evil ones.'

recall *Les Bonnes* because of the sisters' stylized acting and because of obvious *clins d'oeil* in its direction, such as the clock which figures on the mantelpiece in the salon in the first part of the film and which sounds in the play to warn the sisters that they must stop acting out 'la cérémonie' before Madame returns. More generally, avant-garde theatre clearly informs the film, one critic going as far as to say that Papatakis has given the cinema what Beckett in *En attendant Godot* and Ionesco in *Les Chaises* gave to the theatre (Bory 1963). Hailed by Sartre as 'la première tragédie du cinéma'[7] (1963), *Les Abysses* is equally reminiscent of classical theatre in that it adheres to the unities of time—the events take place in one evening; action—from the first the drama centres on ownership of a farm; and place—the whole play is situated in the farmhouse and its yard.

Whilst Genet concentrates on the female characters, Papatakis bases his drama around the family, providing us with the picture of Monsieur which is so often missing from other reproductions of the Papin case. Monsieur Lapeyre, played by Paul Bonifas, is the weak and conciliatory, bordering on cowardly, petty bourgeois owner of a run-down farm situated in *la France profonde* of La Réole, near Bordeaux. He is on his second marriage to Madame, played by Colette Régis, who is even less sympathetic than her husband, and has a daughter, Mademoiselle Elisabeth, played by Pascale de Boysson, by his previous marriage. Mademoiselle has returned home to her father after her own marriage has run into problems. Unlike her father and stepmother, she is decidedly left-wing and has modelled her own character on that of the stereotypical Christian martyr of which she is clearly a parody. The family is the paragon of bourgeois Frenchness in the sense in which Barthes uses the term in *Mythologies*: Monsieur and Madame are *viticulteurs* (wine-growers)—wine being the life blood of France—and they return home in a Citroën Diane—that epitome of French cars (which, incidentally, crops up again nearly thirty years later in *La Cérémonie*). The source of the conflict is that the two maids, Michèle, the eldest, and her younger sister, Marie-Louise, have not received any wages for the past three years because of the financial crisis in which the family finds itself. The fact that they have not been paid has led to their moral and physical degradation and things go from bad to worse once it is revealed that the family intends to sell the farm and the sisters are to be let go with nothing.

The plot outline can thus be read as a political comment on the state of the bourgeoisie. The dilapidated condition of the farm is mirrored by

---

[7] 'the first tragedy of cinema.'

the crumbling of the bourgeois institution of marriage. The nuclear family is falling apart (although by the time we come to Chabrol's film it will have reconstructed itself as we shall see) and who owns what in terms of land and property is of the essence. That both masters and servants claim equal rights to the farm has led the film to be viewed as a metaphor for the Algerian war of independence, and the fact that the maids (unlike their real life counterparts) aspire to land and property ownership does indeed seem to place the film at the centre of debates surrounding colonialism. It is no longer enough for the sisters to be paid in arrears (which would mean remaining in the subservient position) or to settle for something else (which would mean losing their home). When Madame suggests that they can be paid off when the farm is sold and can then buy their own smallholding, they fly into a rage and when Monsieur, finally at the end of his tether because of the sisters' behaviour, goes to get enough money to pay them (which suggests that he could have paid them all along) Michèle responds angrily by hurling bottles and other objects at him. From the outset one of her fears has been that the family will pay them off and they will be denied part of the farm which they have come to see as their right. Much of their energy throughout the film is devoted to scuppering the chances of a sale—they systematically go about wrecking the house, they sabotage the year's harvest by flooding the cellar with wine (thus losing the family one million francs because the wine was to be included in the sale), and they tell the family that the house is invaded by termites, which is later revealed to be fictitious.

The situation remains in the balance while Elisabeth refuses to return to her husband and therefore still has an interest in not selling the farm. She is in a pivotal position between the two couples: Monsieur and Madame, on the one hand, and the two maids on the other, and it is this which has identified her with the left in the French colonial debate. Although she clearly belongs to the bourgeoisie—she returns home and, in a sentimental speech to the two maids, she lists them along with other aspects of her 'property', such as her plane trees, the house, the living room, and her piano—she also has socialist pretensions. This is nowhere better illustrated than in the speech she gives at the dinner table at which both the family and the maids are present. She states that no one is born to be a servant and that equality must be encouraged. She even goes as far as to say that she will share the farm with the maids once it becomes hers after her father's death. In a sense, however, her speech is a parody of the left-wing values that it promotes and her middle of the road approach is politically untenable. Mistrusted and maltreated by the sisters, she is also blamed for their behaviour by her parents and she is mercilessly beaten by her father for being a degenerate and betraying her class.

Whilst Monsieur blames Elisabeth, the visitors who come to buy the farm make it clear that Monsieur is really to blame for the devastation they find in the kitchen once the sisters have killed Madame and Elisabeth. He is accused of being a coward by one of the men present and told that he is the real murderer. However, although it is clear that Monsieur is at fault, it is not clear why this is the case. On the one hand, the implication is that if he had paid the maids their wages and not treated them as slaves, they would not have been reduced to behaving like animals; on the other, it is possible to suggest that he should have taken a firmer hand with the sisters and put a stop to their bad behaviour before it went out of control. We are reminded here of the actual event when Monsieur Lancelin failed to dismiss Christine and Léa after they had been to the mayor complaining of persecution. This would seem to suggest, as in the real affair, that the situation has been provoked because of a lack of a dominant father figure.

The final sequence of the film leads us into even more ambiguous territory. We view Monsieur turning on the light in the kitchen—only his face is illuminated and looking straight at us. This then is the face of the criminal (and it is framed as if about to be shot by a police camera—he therefore replaces the Papin sisters in the 'after' picture). Monsieur then looks down at the bodies as do the three visitors—two men and a woman. However, the final image, a freeze frame, has all four characters looking directly at the spectator—it is therefore the audience, members of the bourgeoisie and we amongst them, who stand accused: they become the jury and we the judged. The audience/spectator is therefore implicated in the affair in a way in which the reader of the written accounts of the case is not.

Although this would seem to imply that the tragedy could have been avoided if society had been different, from its opening sequence the film itself suggests that the outcome could not have been otherwise, for the tension depicted in the first image simply builds throughout making the outcome inevitable. As Sartre rightly says: 'La partie est perdue d'avance pour tous les personnages puisqu'ils sont tous damnés; il faut la jouer pourtant, de bout en bout, jusqu'au double assassinat final, prédit dès la première image, prémédité, inattendu'[8] (1963). Everything, he says, progresses towards 'la catastrophe ultime qui est le moteur immobile du

---

[8] 'The game is lost from the outset for all the characters concerned because they are all damned; they have to play their part, however, from beginning to end, until the final double killing, predicted from the first image, premeditated, yet unexpected.'

film entier'⁹ (1963). The film, which gathers momentum of its own accord, is powered by the relationship between the characters and this paradoxically suggests that it is the interaction between them on a personal rather than a political level which leads to the final tragedy. Again, the film text explores the way in which the balance of power is constantly shifting between the so-called 'masters' and 'slaves' who often step outside their designated roles in personal terms: on a personal level the 'master' is often weak and the 'slave' is often strong.

The strength in the supposedly weaker party is demonstrated from the outset in the opening image to which Sartre refers. It shows the face of Michèle and part of her hand which is holding a hat pin. Her eyes are lowered towards something which she is gouging out and which we cannot see; only the movement of her mouth betrays her concentration and her emotion. The hat pin immediately evokes the gouging out of the eyes of the real event, echoes of which are found throughout the film such as when Marie-Louise is removing the eyes of a potato with a knife. The next image in the opening sequence is that of Marie-Louise who picks up a piece of a broken mirror into which she looks and starts applying eyeliner to her eyes. Once again the idea of the eye being split open is brought to the fore and the film, it seems, pays homage not only to the event but also to Buñuel and Dali's *Un Chien andalou* in whose opening sequence a woman's eye is slit with a razor. In the latter, once the eye has been split open, images of the unconscious come pouring out. What follows in *Les Abysses* is the overflowing of all that has been repressed in the sisters.

The fact that it is a broken mirror in which Marie-Louise sees her fragmented image points to the sisters' mental state. In Lacanian terms they have not reached the mirror stage: they are unable to see a unitary image reflected in the mirror. They therefore remain in the Imaginary and as such have not gained access to the Law of the Father and all that it entails. This is made more explicit by the dialogue in the first part of the film which is fragmented and does not lead to a clear picture of what is going on. Only slowly is the spectator able to build up a picture of the state of affairs: that the sisters have not been paid for three years and that Elisabeth has signed over part of her inheritance to them in the shape of the chicken coop and the outbuildings but that they fear for the validity of this and believe that the master will sell. Apart from the fragmented language, other indications that they are unsocialized are apparent—they are filthy and have no control over their emotions and their affections, which oscillate between love and hate for each other, as

⁹ 'the ultimate catastrophe which is the immobile motor of the whole film.'

indeed do the sentiments between the maids in Genet's play. The film suggests that they are unable to negotiate the Oedipus phase because of the absence of a strong father figure—Monsieur is decidedly weak and it is rather Madame, the usurper within the household (it can be no coincidence that her name is Gertrude making the set-up a kind of inverted *Hamlet* scenario), who seems to hold the power. She also represents the bad breast along with her stepdaughter Elisabeth who oscillates between the functions of the Kleinian good and bad breast.

In fact, the sisters' triangular relationship with Elisabeth adds another interesting dimension to the theme of property and ownership on the level of interpersonal relations. Their relationship with her replicates the relationship which they have between themselves: she is at once loved and hated, desired and abhorred. So again the film explores the young mistress's role in the affair which the written accounts tend to overlook. For her own part, Elisabeth is clearly infatuated with the younger of the two sisters, Marie-Louise, and this infuriates Michèle, usually the more dominant of the two sisters. She interestingly has a phonetically androgynous name which helps to highlight the masculine and (stereotypically) dominant part of her nature and she clearly wants to keep her sister for herself.

That the sisters' relationship is sexual is, if not explicit, then implicit. When they go out to the chicken coop to collect eggs for the crêpes they snuggle together in the straw which recalls the clichéd image of lovers in a haystack. Here the balance of power is shared: at first Michèle assumes the dominant role as Marie-Louise rests her head upon her shoulder; then they switch positions and Marie-Louise lends her shoulder to Michèle. It is this relationship which Elisabeth threatens and which infuriates Michèle who warns her sister of Elisabeth's intentions as they lie there in the straw. When Elisabeth comes to join them, Michèle guards their space ferociously; on the surface she is protecting her property—the chicken coop—but at a deeper level she is guarding her sister for herself.

For her part, Elisabeth is torn between mothering Marie-Louise and desiring her sexually. This is clear from the dinner table scene. Michèle, who is irritated by the attentions which Elisabeth is bestowing upon her sister, leaves the room throwing Marie-Louise into a panic. In order to stop her screaming, Elisabeth pops a spoonful of stew into her mouth which Marie-Louise spits out at her. The good mother's breast has been rejected. Elisabeth then begins to eat Marie-Louise's bread. That the bread is associated with Marie-Louise's body is clear when the three women meet outside after the meal. Michèle accuses Elisabeth of wanting to partake of Holy Communion (by eating the bread/body of her sister) and goes on to whisper obscenities in her ear after which she incites Marie-Louise to hit Elisabeth and, in a state of arousal, then does the same.[10]

That sex and violence, normally the prerogative of men, are clearly associated here is made all the more apparent by the scenes which lead up to the killings and the killings themselves. What ultimately drives the sisters to murder is not so much the fact that they lose the smallholding (the chance had gone once Elisabeth managed to wrestle the rights from Michèle when she first heard that the property had been sold) but the fact that Elisabeth, reconciled with her husband, threatens to have the sisters put in a convent where they would be separated. The text here is obviously drawing on the real Papin story and the fact that the sisters were placed in a religious house of correction by their mother. In the film this threat leads to their final degradation; the one sprawled legs akimbo over the stove, the other at her feet with her skirt around her thighs, and it is thus that Madame, Elisabeth, and the woman visitor find them. Elisabeth now makes her fatal mistake: she walks over to Marie-Louise and pulls her skirt down to hide her modesty. This gesture is interpreted as sexual by Michèle, who attacks Elisabeth in a move which is at once violent and sexually charged. She bites her neck thus partaking of the Holy Communion which she formerly used as a sexual insult; she is biting into the bread/body and vampiristically going for blood/wine (the theme of vampirism will be more fully explored in relation to *Sister my Sister*). At the same time she is metaphorically biting the bad breast. She then penetrates her victim as she stabs her with the kitchen knife. Her sister joins in the frenzy, picks up the iron, an obvious reference to the iron which blew the fuse in the Lancelin household, and bludgeons Madame, the usurping mother, to death. What is especially interesting here is that the only witness of the event which in reality had no witnesses is a woman—the visitor. It is she who calls out to the men, who only arrive to view the scene once the carnage is over. The film therefore ends with a woman as the only authority (apart from the spectator that is) on what 'really' happened. Women and violence, it seems, are to remain beyond the ken of men.

Whilst *Les Abysses* is clearly concerned with a political situation which is particularly pertinent to the time in which it is set, it is also an exploration of the personal factors which resulted in the Papin murders and

---

[10] It is interesting that Elisabeth masochistically takes this beating and is not deterred by it. She is only reconciled with her husband once she has been beaten by her father—it is he who imposes the Law of the Father on his daughter and momentarily puts her sexuality back on the heterosexual straight and narrow.

therefore draws not only on the sisters' relationship with each other but also with their young mistress, (Geneviève Lancelin, we remember, was Christine Papin's age), which is not explored by most of the written reproductions. In *La Cérémonie* the young mistress becomes instrumental in provoking the situation that will lead to the murders as we shall see.

Claude Chabrol's *La Cérémonie*

Whilst Chabrol does not admit that *La Cérémonie* is directly based on the Papin affair, it nevertheless influenced the psychoanalyst, Caroline Eliacheff, the co-writer with Chabrol of *La Cérémonie*, when she was adapting the novel on which the film is based, Ruth Rendell's *A Judgement in Stone* (Austin: 1999). The film's title also refers us to the Papin sisters since 'la cérémonie' is the name the maids in Genet's *Les Bonnes* give to their role-playing in which they continually try to work up to killing Madame. However, it is to two other films called *The Ceremony* that Chabrol maintains he is paying homage—those of Laurence Harvey (1963) and Oshima (1971), both of which deal with public executions (Berthomieu, Jeancolas, and Vassé 1995: 9). The killings in Chabrol's film are therefore equated with an execution, which also refers us to the real affair and the fact that Christine was initially sentenced to the guillotine. Intentionally or not, therefore, *La Cérémonie* is indebted to the Papin affair, which in the film becomes the paradigm for tensions existing in contemporary society.

In *La Cérémonie*, the two sisters are replaced by a maid, Sophie Bonhomme, played by Sandrine Bonnaire, and her friend, the postmistress Jeanne, played by Isabelle Huppert. Sophie is taken on by the Lelièvres, an upper middle-class family, based on the traditional nuclear family which was seen to be breaking up in *Les Abysses* but which has reconstituted itself here in the form of a second marriage between Monsieur Lelièvre, an industrialist played by Jean-Pierre Cassel, and Madame, an ex-model played by Jacqueline Bisset. They live together with her teenage son, Gilles, played by Valentin Merlet, and are visited periodically by his daughter, Melinda, played by Virginie Ledoyen, who is a student. Their large house is situated near St Malo in Brittany, which although not *la France profonde*, is still resolutely provincial.

For the most part, Chabrol draws heavily on the main characters of Rendell's text which refers openly to the Papin sisters, although they are somewhat curiously brought to the fore through a process of denial. In evoking the two protagonists, the narrator of *A Judgement in Stone* says that 'the relationship between Eunice Parchman and Joan Smith was never of a lesbian nature. They bore no resemblance to the Papin sisters, who, while cook and housemaid to a mother and daughter in Le Mans, murdered their employers in 1933' (Rendell 1994: 72). Coming as it does right at the beginning of chapter 9 and just over a third of the way through the novel, the denial of the likeness only makes the similarities between the two sets of women all the more apparent. It is also interesting that Rendell evokes the Papin sisters in order to deny that the relationship between Eunice Parchman, the servant, and Joan Smith, her friend, was of a lesbian nature. At this point in the text, there is no evidence to suggest that it is. Joan Smith is even given a hen-pecked husband. Eunice, we are told, only resembles the Papins in that she is female and a servant; as for her sexuality 'she was an almost sexless being, without normal or abnormal desires' (1994: 72). The implication here is that lesbianism is abnormal and in the case of Joan Smith it does account in part for her deviance, for whilst Eunice, 'for all her adventurous wanderings, did not know what lesbianism was, Joan Smith certainly knew and had very likely experimented with it, as she had experimented with most things' (1994: 72).

If Rendell plays down the possibility of a sexual relationship between Eunice and Joan, Chabrol evokes it without making it over explicit. He has replaced the frumpy 48-year-old Eunice Parchman and the bird-like 50-year-old Joan Smith with the young and attractive figures of Sandrine Bonnaire as the maid, Sophie Bonhomme, and Isabelle Huppert, cast out of type for once, as her friend, the *postière* (postmistress), Jeanne. This was deliberately done to make the characters more appealing to the audience and to get away from a Eunice figure, who in Chabrol's words is 'une espèce de chose gelatineuse',[11] and a Joan character who is too typically English (Berthomieu, Jeancolas, and Vassé 1995: 8). He does, however, try to retain a certain Englishness in his choice of Jacqueline Bisset as the mistress of the house, and in locating the film in Brittany and therefore relatively near to England (Berthomieu, Jeancolas, and Vassé 1995: 8).

The two friends, Sophie and Jeanne, are not only a lot younger than Eunice and Joan but are often portrayed as young girls rather than women. Sophie has a passion for chocolate and Jeanne wears her hair in pigtails and dresses in short skirts of the type which little girls normally wear. The only relationship they have is with each other. There are no

---

[11] 'some sort of gelatinous object.'

men in their lives other than Monsieur Lelièvre, Gilles, and the priest of
the *secours catholique* (catholic aid charity). In this they are certainly like
the Papin sisters who never had or sought any suitors. The only other
male with whom Sophie comes into contact is the man who delivers
the groceries. She is totally unresponsive to his flirtatious remarks and
simply relieved when on the pretence of helping her to sign for the order
he takes her hand and moves the pen for her. His remark that she should
give him a call if she should 'need anything' is taken at face value and
when he leaves Sophie gives him no more thought and simply returns
to her vacuuming. It is only in Jeanne's company that Sophie comes
alive: that the 'pierre' (stone), Sophie, starts to become more like her
friend the 'papillon' (butterfly), Jeanne (De Bruyn 1995). As their relationship progresses, physical contact between them increases, although
it is never overtly sexual, and Sophie begins to dress more like her friend.
From wearing her hair either loose or in a ponytail, she wears plaited
pigtails like Jeanne's, and from buttoned-up shirts she changes into
V-necked cardigans and short skirts. When Jeanne invites Sophie to stay
with her when she leaves the family, she does so kneeling on her bed with
her legs slightly apart. There is only one bed in her small *deux pièces*
(two-roomed flat) and the implication is clear. However, their sexuality
is not presented as a mature sexuality, but instead as a childish sexuality, reminiscent of the relationship existing between the two teenage girls
in *Heavenly Creatures* (1994), before it becomes a fully-fledged affair.

What is also clear is that women who kill are somehow not real, mature
women. They are immature and irresponsible creatures. This is most
evident in *La Cérémonie* in the scene where the two 'girls' (and here it
is appropriate to call them girls rather than women, for if such an
appellation robs them of their credibility as women, this is going no
further than the film itself has already gone) are helping to sort out
second-hand clothes for the poor. They are set apart from the 'real'
women who are all standing at tables sorting the clothes. Jeanne and
Sophie, in contrast, are kneeling on the floor discarding clothes which
are no good by flinging them over their shoulders, and making jokes at
the same time about the priest.

In *La Cérémonie* the friends' delinquency also revolves around two
other factors—literacy (or the lack of it) and successful access to the
symbolic order of language. It is this which permits a reworking of the
class struggle which for many underpinned the Papin affair, and indeed Chabrol has called his film 'le dernier film marxiste' (Guérin
and Taboulay 1997: 68). He says that he finds it ludicrous that the
class struggle is deemed by some to have fallen with the Berlin Wall
(Berthomieu, Jeancolas, and Vassé 1995: 9). For him, class is still very

much an issue and one of the ways in which he explores class inequality in *La Cérémonie* is by examining the discrepancies in power that culture affords in a society which is supposed to have democratized access to culture. The film shows cultural democracy to be merely an illusion with hierarchies in the cultural domain helping to maintain class barriers. What is important, therefore, is not only the power that results from the inequality of the classes in a material sense but also in a cultural sense: whoever owns and has access to the dominant aspects of culture such as language and high culture, as opposed to popular culture, also holds the power. The Papin case can therefore be seen to act as a model for exploring issues which are particularly pertinent in French society today.

The same tension between popular and high culture also exists at the heart of Chabrol's 'hypotexte', to borrow Genette's term (1982: 11), *A Judgement in Stone*, a work which, since it is a crime novel, belongs to the category of popular fiction. However, the novel also draws on texts belonging to high culture and the resulting tension parallels conflicts existing between the classes. The novel's title itself is a reference to the Don Juan tale (in that the statue of the Commendatore finally judges Don Juan). It was first written by Tirso di Molina in 1630 and has since become one of the main myths of Western culture: everyone knows who Don Juan is and indeed the term Don Juan has become part of our everyday vocabulary. However, despite this familiarity, the reference to him contained within Rendell's title is unlikely to be recognized by those unfamiliar with reproductions of the Don Juan myth now belonging to high culture such as Molière's play, *Dom Juan* (1665) or Mozart's opera, *Don Giovanni* (1787), which is evoked and indeed acts as a metatext within the novel and *La Cérémonie*. In a sense, therefore, both Rendell's novel and Chabrol's film help to bridge the gap between high and low culture, by making aspects of high culture, in this instance Mozart's *Don Giovanni*, available to consumers of popular culture. Both text and film can therefore be seen as indicative of the trend towards a democratization of culture whilst at the same time exploring the mechanisms which are still in place to prevent this from happening.

In *La Cérémonie* the friends' delinquency also revolves around two other factors—literacy (or the lack of it) and successful access to the symbolic order of language. Both women fail in this area: Sophie because she cannot read, Jeanne because she reads indiscriminately including other people's mail; the one cannot go far enough, the other goes too far. Their position in relation to the written word reminds us that the Papin sisters were no great readers. At their trial the judge concluded that their crime could not have been inspired by their reading material, since they read nothing except some religious works. He is reported to have said to them: 'Vous n'aviez pas, si je puis dire, la tête montée par certaines lectures. On n'a trouvé dans votre chambre que des livres de piété'[12] (Le Guillant 1963: 893). Ironically, in *La Cérémonie*, the reason why Sophie murders the family is that she cannot read. Here the film remains faithful to the Rendell text which begins: 'Eunice Parchman killed the Coverdale family because she could not read or write' (1994: 7). The effect here is added to by the ironic use of Eunice's surname, Parchman being an obvious reference to parchment. The reason why Sophie cannot read is tied in with the fact that she has not gained successful entry to the symbolic order; in Lacanian terms she has not successfully negotiated the mirror-phase. This is made evident in *La Cérémonie* by the way in which Sophie's inability to read the shopping list that Madame Lelièvre has left her is filmed in the mirror. Sophie is unable to negotiate the mirror-phase and pass beyond it into the world of the symbolic. The mirror in the hallway is significant in that it reflects the door to the kitchen which is referred to by Madame as Sophie's 'domain'. In not being able to read, she is kept firmly on that side of the mirror; she is not allowed access to the world of the Lelièvres, from which she is divided not only in terms of class and material wealth, but also in terms of her access to culture.

Hints as to Sophie's inability to read are given from the film's outset (Berthomieu, Jeancolas, and Vassé 1995). The opening sequence shows Sophie asking a passer-by where a café is despite the fact that it is clearly visible in front of her. Later, in a scene reminiscent of Hitchcock, Madame goes to the station to meet Sophie from the 9 a.m. train only to find she is not on it. Sophie then appears on the other platform as if out of nowhere. Her mistake is easily explained by her saying that she caught an earlier train. The spectator is given a more significant clue as to Sophie's problem when she stops abruptly short of the threshold of the library and will not venture beyond it when Madame is showing her around the house. However, the first time the spectator becomes fully aware of Sophie's illiteracy is when Madame leaves her a note on the kitchen table. Unable to read what it says, Sophie runs upstairs to her room and gets out a book which resembles a diary with a lock on it and which contains phonetic exercises designed to help identify certain letters. The fact that the book is locked and that she has to open it with a key reveals the extent to which Sophie is ashamed of her inability to

---

[12] 'Your heads hadn't been turned, if I may say so, by certain reading material. Only religious books were found in your room.'

read. Just as an entry into a personal diary must be hidden from prying eyes, so Sophie's 'disability' must be kept secret.

It is because of her inability to read that her friendship with Jeanne develops. Unable to decipher the shopping list which Madame has left for her, Sophie takes it along to the post office and gets Jeanne to phone through the order for her. Sophie has no need to fear Jeanne because Jeanne's form of delinquency, her insatiable inquisitiveness which results in her inability not to read that which does not belong to her, means that she is always prepared to read notes, cards, and letters which are destined for others, including the Lelièvres' mail. This means that she never presses Sophie to read for herself and willingly accepts her excuse of not having her glasses. As far as Jeanne is concerned, Sophie's 'secret' is safe and this of course distinguishes her from the Lelièvre family and Melinda in particular. Believing Sophie's lack of interest in books is due to inadequate eye wear, they insist that she visits the opticians to get new glasses—something which she only pretends to do, coming back with a pair of sunglasses instead. In fact, Melinda's discovery of Sophie's disability is what sets the events leading to the murders in motion.

Somewhat ironically, it is through the metaphor of 'seeing' that the discovery comes to light. Melinda, in an attempt to be friendly, asks Sophie to read aloud the questions of a quiz in a woman's magazine which she says she will answer. After Sophie has fended her off with various excuses, Melinda tries on Sophie's glasses only to discover that they are fake. In assuming fake and tinted glasses, Melinda is able to see clearly that Sophie cannot read. Sophie then blackmails Melinda saying that she will tell Melinda's father that she is pregnant if she dares to reveal her secret (in Rendell's novel one of Eunice Parchman's specialities is blackmail). Melinda, as a good girl should, does the right thing and tells her father who gives Sophie a week to leave. Monsieur Lelièvre here does what Monsieur Lancelin failed to do: he dismisses Sophie after her misdemeanour, whereas Lancelin chose to ignore the sisters' visit to the mayor complaining of persecution. However, like Lancelin, his fate is sealed; action no more than inaction can save the family. Sophie's shame is now complete since the whole family knows that she is illiterate.

The discovery that Sophie cannot read parallels the discovery, again by the Lelièvres, that Jeanne reads their mail. Both women are therefore seen to be deficient. Monsieur says when he dismisses Sophie: 'Ce n'est pas entièrement votre faute',[13] which suggests that it is partly her own fault. The inability to read and the inability to refrain from reading

---

[13] 'it's not entirely your fault.'

are symptoms it seems of the psychotic tendencies which lie beneath the surface in both women (tendencies which Lacan was at pains to reveal in his piece on the Papin sisters) and which have erupted in the past with murderous consequences. Sharing their past misdemeanours with each other helps to cement their friendship. Jeanne, we are told, was accused of killing her child, and Sophie, it is suggested, killed her bedridden father. Both women realize that they are responsible for these respective crimes (even though Jeanne was acquitted) and that in each case there was not enough evidence to convict them. They therefore have a background in murder and this makes the way in which their friendship gains momentum and finally spirals out of control all the more sinister. Guy Austin has identified their similar background as contributing to a 'fusion of identities between Sophie and Jeanne as if, like the Papin sisters, they were turning into a murderous third person' (1999: 151).

The murders themselves take place against the backdrop of Mozart's opera, *Don Giovanni*, and the master–servant dialectic, of which the Papin affair has become a cultural paradigm, is played out here on two different levels: in the relationship between the Don and his manservant, Leporello, and between the Lelièvres and Sophie and Jeanne. Furthermore, the opera acts as a metatext for what happens in the film. Chabrol considered deviating from Rendell's text and using *The Marriage of Figaro* instead. However, he realized that this would be impossible without altering the progression of events and therefore decided to remain faithful to *A Judgement in Stone* (Berthomieu, Jeancolas, and Vassé 1995: 11). In the film, the 'ceremony' to which the title refers takes place in more ways than one. Firstly, it operates on the level of the Lelièvres' activities: they are dressed for dinner and for the opera which follows and which they are going to watch on the television. Again the discrepancy between high and low culture and its accessibility comes to the fore. The television, which acts as the medium of transmission and despite the fact that it is presented as being available to both classes (Sophie has the Lelièvres' old set in her room), nevertheless plays a key role in keeping the classes apart. This is clearly seen by the use to which it is put by Sophie as opposed to members of the family: Sophie happily zaps through the channels and watches things indiscriminately, but when Gilles does likewise on the family's 'new toy', a satellite TV, he is admonished by Monsieur who says he would rather watch a good sunset. The programmes to which Sophie has access because of her position within the cultural hierarchy (and here the difference between what is accessible and what is available is very evident), simply serve to keep her in her place within the social hierarchy, the implication being that they have a brutalizing effect. The family members, on the other hand, are able to access high culture because of their position within the social, and by extension, cultural hierarchy. The ending of *La Cérémonie*, therefore, is as much about the clash between low culture and high culture as it is about one class wreaking revenge on the other.

The first two chords of the overture of *Don Giovanni* sound as the family settle down to watch the opera. The second chord, in D minor, which is the dominant chord of the music (and therefore perhaps heralds what is to come), is heard as the scene shifts to Sophie and Jeanne making their way to the house in Jeanne's car. No further music is heard from the overture. When the girls arrive at the house the music from Act 1, scene 19 fades in. Don Giovanni is hosting a ball and Don Ottavio, his fiancée, Donna Anna (whose father Don Giovanni has killed), and Donna Elvira (abandoned by Don Giovanni) arrive in masks to reveal Don Giovanni's misdeeds. It is evident that Sophie and Jeanne are identified with the women who are from the same social stratum as the Don on whom they are seeking vengeance. As for Monsieur, he is clearly identified with the Don. Interestingly, this indicates that the balance of power between master and servant within the Lelièvre household has shifted: Sophie is no longer in the subservient position for she is not in the Lelièvres' employ. Having entered the house via the gunroom, Sophie and Jeanne go into the kitchen where Sophie makes some hot chocolate, prefiguring Leporello's call for chocolate in scene 20. Here Sophie is clearly identified with Leporello, although the person she is serving is Jeanne and not Monsieur Lelièvre. This in turn is a comment on the balance of power in the relationship between Sophie and Jeanne at this point.

Scene 20 begins as the girls leave the kitchen and start making their way up the main staircase. On the first landing, Jeanne, who is carrying the tray, leads Sophie into the Lelièvres' bedroom where Jeanne's obsession with Madame Lelièvre comes to the fore. Here the character of Jeanne is clearly reminiscent of Lacan's 'Aimée' (Marguerite Pantaine), the *postière* who tried to kill the prominent actress Huguette Duflos in 1931 (in the film Madame used to be a successful model). Jeanne's need to defile Madame's bedroom unmasks Jeanne's ambiguous feelings towards her, based as they are on sexual desire and murderous intent. She announces that the Lelièvres have been screwing, smashes the photograph first of Madame and then of Monsieur, jumps on to the bed, and pours the hot chocolate from the jug which she pretends is a penis from which she is urinating. She then goes to the wardrobe and begins tearing up Madame's clothes with Sophie following suit in a mounting kind of *folie à deux*, reminiscent of the *délire* which clearly overcame the

Papin sisters with Léa catching her sister's madness as it were. Again Sophie and Jeanne's actions find their reflection in the opera as one of the characters throws a cape on to the floor. The balance of power is now clearly inverted. As the family continues watching the opera, Sophie and Jeanne look down on them from above like gods pondering their victims below. The Lelièvres, who enjoy the sport of hunting, now become the hares who are going to be hunted (*le lièvre* in French meaning hare— perhaps a covert reference to the fact that the Papins were initially called Lapins by the press).

Once downstairs again, Sophie asks Jeanne in an almost nonchalant way what they should do next and Jeanne, yawning, replies almost as nonchalantly that they should perhaps scare the family. This suggests that the events which follow are not so much planned as simply spiralling out of control, which makes the crime seem essentially motiveless. Here the film has definite affinities with the Papin killings which were deemed to lack a sufficient motive and it is partly this which has made the case so unfathomable. In *La Cérémonie* Jeanne takes the lead once more in that she cuts the telephone cord and takes one of the guns off the wall but it is Sophie who knows how to load it. By this time Act 1 of the opera has finished and the family take coffee in the interval. They hear a noise which Madame identifies as the 'postière' and Monsieur goes to investigate just as Act 2 begins. In the opera Leporello is singing that he wants to leave Don Giovanni because the latter nearly had him killed in identifying him as Zerlina's assailant and Don Giovanni is trying to reassure Leporello that it was only a joke. When Monsieur arrives in the kitchen, Jeanne pretends to shoot him and he demands that the women put down the guns and grabs the barrel of the one Jeanne is holding, in a move which is reminiscent of Hilbert's victim in *Érostrate*. Sophie then shoots Monsieur, first from a distance and then moves towards him and shoots him again. He is shot just as the Don is singing 'you are mad' and Leporello sings 'no no no' over and over again. Contrary to the opera, where Don Giovanni successfully persuades Leporello to stay with him by paying him, Sophie repays Monsieur by shooting him. In the one, the master triumphs over the servant, in the other the servant triumphs over the master.

The tables have also turned with regard to the relationship between Sophie and Jeanne. Up until this point Jeanne has been the leader, now Sophie becomes the dominant one; on one level, she is the Don to Jeanne's Leporello, and on another she is the Don to Jeanne's Elvira. It is at this point too that the 'ceremony' of the title, in terms of what the two friends deliberately act out as an execution, begins. The friends here succeed in doing what Genet's maids failed to do in their 'ceremony', that is, kill the other rather than the self (Claire in *Les Bonnes* of course commits suicide). They also set themselves apart from the Papin sisters who, as far as can be surmised, killed without premeditation.

The 'ceremony' is filmed in such a way as to parody the genre of the western. The two women slug down coffee as if it were whisky at the bar and move with the guns towards the rest of the family. As they do so, there is a jump in the opera to Act 2, scene 3, and the Canzonetta. The Don and his manservant have exchanged clothes in order that the Don can serenade Elvira's maid. He accompanies himself on a mandolin (an unusual instrument for the time) and as he sings 'Deh! Vieni alla finestra, o mio tesoro',[14] Madame Lelièvre moves towards the window. Roles are again inverted: the master (Don Giovanni), as his servant (Leporello), is serenading the mistress (Madame Lelièvre), who in the opera is a maid (Elvira's maid). Gilles is then sent to investigate the noise which sounds like a car backfiring (and which he jokingly refers to as Monsieur shooting the women). As Gilles moves towards the doors of the *salon* they swing open, like the doors of a saloon, and the two women enter and shoot Gilles just as the Don sings: 'Davanti agli occhi tuoi morir vogl'io.'[15] As the Don assumes the position of the servant in the opera, so the women assume the position of the masters. They then immediately shoot Melinda in the stomach, followed by Madame to the singing of the next two lines which betray the sexual elements of the killings: 'Tu ch'hai la bocca dolce più del miele',[16] 'Tu che il zucchero porti in mezzo al core'.[17] The sexual overtures of the relationship between the two women and their mistresses which are highlighted here were significantly absent from many of the early reproductions of the Papin case. They are, however, fully explored in *Sister my Sister* as we shall see. Having killed the women, Sophie turns and shoots the books on the shelf, and in so doing kills off the symbolic order to which she does not and cannot belong.

In one sense the obvious reference to the genre of the western with the women in the role of cowboys brandishing phallic symbols means that once again the act of killing is appropriated as a masculine deed. The film seems to be saying that if young women such as Sophie and Jeanne kill, they have to do it as if they were men, they cannot do it as women. The use of rifles also 'normalizes' or 'heterosexualizes' the sexual overtones of the killing of the two women. The film seems to shy away from lesbian implications here. The disavowal of lesbianism is in fact brought about by the killings themselves, in much the same way as the 'passage

---

[14] 'Come to the window, my treasure.'   [15] 'I want to die before your eyes.'
[16] 'Your mouth is sweeter than honey.'   [17] 'Your heart houses sweet desires.'

à l'acte' for Dupré marked the end of the Papin sisters' incestuous relationship. This is made clear after the murders have taken place. Sophie
stands on the side and leans on her rifle (she is therefore still invested
with a penis) and Jeanne, without her gun, approaches her like a woman
in a saloon going up to her mate. She leans against her and brushes
the hair from her face as the Don sings 'Lasciati almen veder, mio bel-
l'amore!',[18] highlighting the fact that the act is a sexually charged one, but
now it signifies heterosexuality and difference, rather than homosexuality and sameness which was characteristic of the women's relationship
before the murders. Sophie here is clearly in the dominant 'male' role
with Jeanne in the 'female' role.

The calm which follows the killings is chilling as Sophie's 'Ça va'
('good') is echoed by Jeanne's barely inflected 'on a bien fait (?)',[19] recalling the Papin sisters' 'en voilà du propre'.[20] Jeanne leaves Sophie, who
reverts to type, to clean up just as the Papin sisters cleaned up after the
deed was done.

In the end, however, it is literally the Law of the Father which triumphs
(over Jeanne at least) in that the priest or 'père' accidentally drives his
car into Jeanne's car killing her outright. The divine it seems has also
intervened here recalling the opera's ending where the statue of the
Commendatore triumphs over Don Giovanni. The forces of law and
order also seem to prevail when the policeman at the accident scene
switches on Melinda's tape recorder which Jeanne took with her when
she left the house and on which Melinda had been recording the opera.
Don Giovanni's voice rings out, followed by the shots, followed by the
girls' final words. The implication is that the powers that be which
uphold the status quo of both class and culture have the information
they need to restore order.

What is not clear, however, is whether Sophie will be apprehended
since she is last seen walking off into the night (thus repeating her flight
after killing her father). The final words of the film, 'On a bien fait (?)',
which constitute the true ending of the film (the credits having begun
rolling just as Sophie approaches the accident scene unnoticed), are
what ultimately remain with the spectator. The final triumph is therefore
the women's.

In *La Cérémonie* the killings can be seen to work on several different
levels. They therefore take on a polyvalency equivalent to the Papin affair
and this serves to reinforce the undecidability of the crime. On a basic
level, the family's murder represents the lower classes overcoming the

---

[18] 'At least let me see you, my beloved.'   [19] 'we did well/did we do well/the right thing (?)'
[20] 'what a mess.'

higher classes—the implosion to which Chabrol referred. It also signifies the triumph of popular culture (the ceremony acted out in the genre of the western) over high culture (the opera). Seen in terms of gender, women kill men, by whom they have traditionally been repressed, and at the same time they kill women, who are both 'other' in terms of their class, and 'the same' in terms of their gender. Yet in killing both the men and the women, they are codified as men so that the violence emerges as both masculine and heterosexual. A very different picture emerges in *Sister my Sister* as we shall now see.

Nancy Meckler's *Sister my Sister*

Nancy Meckler's *Sister my Sister* (1994) is a British production which was filmed in Pinewood Studios, London, and in Amiens, France. The screenplay was written by Wendy Kesselman and is clearly an adaptation of her text, *My Sister in this House*. The film was screened as part of the New York Lesbian and Gay Film Festival in 1995 and focuses its attention on the relationships between the sisters and their mistresses. However, this is not to say that issues of class have been ignored—which in any case would have been impossible given the subject-matter—and they do in fact play a role as Christine Coffman in her reading of the film makes clear (1999), although much of what she says is even more applicable to *My Sister in this House*.

Sister my Sister differs from *Les Abysses* and *La Cérémonie* not only because it is made by a woman but also because it deliberately focuses on what the Papin trial sought to establish and what many subsequent readings, in particular those of Lacan and Dupré, deny, and that is that the relationship between the sisters was an overtly incestuous one (de Lauretis 1998: 869; Coffman 1999: 334). *Sister my Sister* confronts both incest and lesbianism full on. Like *Les Bonnes* and *My Sister in this House*, it relies on an all-female cast, consisting of Christine and Lea, played by Joely Richardson and Jodhi May respectively, of Madame Danzard (Madame Lancelin), played by Julie Walters and of her daughter Isabelle Danzard (Geneviève Lancelin), played by Sophie Thursfield. The world in which the action takes place is an almost exclusively female one and this creates a sense of claustrophobia which is added to by the fact that most of the action takes place indoors; the windows are either obscured by lace curtains or they simply reflect the sisters inside the house. Men are noticeable by their absence—Madame is a widow and Isabelle is unmarried—and then by their presence, firstly as a gaze and then as a voice. The gaze is that of the photographer who is obscured by his camera and the voices are those of the priest (who can be heard in the background when the sisters are in church) and of the magistrates at the trial which exist in terms of the voice-over in the closing sequences. Men are never actually 'seen', nor are their voices mentioned in the cast list at the end of the film and so they are doubly effaced. Whilst in one sense this upholds the traditional roles allocated to males (as voice and gaze), it also reassesses traditional male discourse in that women often assume positions which in the past have been the sole preserve of men.

The re-examination of traditional male discourse is evident right from the outset of the film, which cries out for a psychoanalytic reading, beginning as it does with flashbacks in black and white which are interspersed with the opening credits. The film therefore begins by interpreting the childhood of the Papin sisters upon which many reproductions of the affair have also dwelt. We see a little girl mothering her younger sister (the girls, incidentally, are played by the real sisters Gabriella and Aimée Schmidt); she washes her, feeds her, and brushes her hair. A woman, whom we surmise is the mother, then enters and takes the younger sister away (the film here remains faithful to real life in that Léa was undoubtedly the mother's favourite). We are clearly invited to see this as a metatext for what follows and it does indeed set up relationships which are repeated and mirrored throughout the film. What is evident here is the total absence of men from this triangular situation. In terms of the Oedipus complex, women have been allotted the places which Freud, and later Lacan, accord to males. The younger sister plays the child to the older sister's mother and the mother takes on the role of the father who threatens the dyadic unity of mother and child. In this instance, it is both the child-mother and the child-child who have problems with the separation. Failing to gain the affection of the real mother, the older sister (Christine) turns herself into a mother figure and replays with the younger sister (Lea) that which she wishes she herself has as a child. When the mother enters the room, it is the younger sister, her favourite, whom she takes with her, leaving the older sister alone.

The desperation which Christine feels when she is abandoned is replayed in two further flashbacks in the film (it is interesting that the original flashbacks are in black and white rather than in the blue and white and subdued colours of Christine's reflections). Christine's flashbacks refer to the time she spent in the orphanage (in *My Sister in this House* Lea is given these memories and this makes for a totally different reading). She is waiting for Sister Veronica to come out of a room and when she does so Christine embraces her only to be rebuffed by the nun who walks off down the hall without looking back. The nun's role is threefold: she is a 'sister' ('bonne soeur'—interesting because the sisters are also 'bonnes'), she is a mother figure who refuses the child's advances, and she is also a father figure in that she is named after the saint who gave Christ a handkerchief upon which to wipe his brow and on which his image was left imprinted. She thus has affinities with the male photographer who captures the sisters' image in a photograph and is identified only as a gaze, but here she does not give 'Christ-ine' a second look.

In both instances Christine's flashbacks are replayed immediately after a situation which threatens the sisters's unity. However, they serve not only to demonstrate how the psychological dynamics of the sisters' relationship were established in childhood and are then repeated in adulthood, but also to comment on the sexual tensions which exist between the sisters and their mistresses, something which many reproductions of the affair, including those of Lacan and Dupré, choose to ignore. As Coffman rightly points out, Meckler's film goes some way towards filling the gaps of Lacan's assessment of the Papin case, for Lacan concentrated solely on the sisters without taking the relationship between the sisters and the other two women involved into account (Coffman 1999: 352). Not only that but the scenes surrounding the flashbacks also help to build speculation around the erotic nature of the relationship between mother and daughter (again something upon which many previous reproductions of the Papin case did not dare speculate).

The first flashback occurs after Christine has witnessed a growing closeness between Isabelle and Lea. Isabelle has been dancing alone in the drawing room where Lea is cleaning. She then hands Lea a hairbrush which the latter takes and with which she begins to brush her young mistress's hair. The exchange, which is clearly erotic and is recognized as such by Christine and Madame who witness the event and are both extremely jealous, also replicates the mother–child dyad of the first scene (this time with Lea as the mother and Isabelle as the child) and later the erotic exchanges between Christine and Lea. That Christine and Madame are both jealous can be understood in two ways: firstly, they want to keep their own flesh and blood for themselves; secondly, in Freudian terms, their feelings can be interpreted as a projection of their own desire on to the other women involved. Christine projects her sexual feelings for Isabelle on to Lea and Madame projects her desire for Lea on to her daughter.

Both of the older women (who also mirror each other in that they are onlookers and outsiders) deal with their jealousy in different ways: the one goes to the kitchen and smashes something on the table, the other, after throwing a sweet paper on to the floor and pinching Lea's arm until she picks it up (thus referring us to the famous incident when Madame

Lancelin is said to have pinched Léa's arm until it bled) inspects the cooking and turns off the dripping tap without saying a word to Christine. The one reaction is clearly a repressed version of the other. In firmly replacing the lid on the boiling saucepan and turning off the tap, Madame is putting into check potentially explosive forces; once again order has been restored and emotion has been repressed. Christine is now left alone and the first flashback to Sister Veronica occurs. She has been rejected not only by her sister but also by the mother figure of Madame (again we are reminded that the Papin sisters used to call Madame 'maman' and conversely their mother Madame) both of whom are present in Sister Veronica.

The second time the flashback occurs is after the scene where Isabelle is having a dress fitted. Christine is on her knees pinning up the hem of the dress and Lea is standing and smiling at Isabelle. Christine then ruins the dress by hacking away at the neckline with a pair of scissors in a move which prefigures the eventual mutilating of the bodies (the sexual overtones are made clear especially when one considers that the daughter's legs and buttocks are eventually slashed with a knife). The sisters then run upstairs where Christine's pathological jealousy surfaces once more. She accuses Lea of wanting to go with Isabelle when the latter marries and leaves home (something which, because of Isabelle's relationship with her mother, is very unlikely to happen). The idea of being separated from her sister is certainly too much for her. The flashback to Sister Veronica then occurs for the second time, with Christine explaining to Lea what happened: 'I waited for her and she wouldn't talk to me, she wouldn't turn round.' The fact that Sister Veronica would not talk to her replicates the silence that exists between Madame and the sisters (which in real life is said to have come about between employers and employees after the sisters broke with their mother). The situation is resolved when Lea suggests that she pretends to be Sister Veronica and places a towel over her head to replicate the nun's wimple (in *My Sister in this House* it is Christine who comforts Lea in this way). Christine then buries her face in Lea's lap. Lea has become the mother to Christine's child and the Sister who does not ignore the sister. The image here conjures up the Pietà with Christine this time successfully assuming the role of Christ.

What happens in the scenes which depict the sisters' childhood is re-enacted and finally resolved in adulthood, and the different relationships are played out again and again so that the roles between the four women are always switching. Following the opening credits and the flashbacks in black and white, the scene changes to after the killings have taken place. The camera backs away down a flight of stairs and we see the blood-strewn hall and part of a woman's leg. This is accompanied by the tune 'Sleep my little Sister Sleep'. A relationship between the two little girls in black and white and what happened on the stairs is immediately set up. What that relationship is exactly we do not know but the tune reminds us that the girls and the dead woman are in a sense all sisters. In retrospect, we know that the little girls are the maids and the two bodies (we only see part of one here) are those of Madame Danzard and her daughter. From the very beginning, therefore, the film establishes a parity between the maids and their employers and throughout the film the relationships which exist between the women act very much like a hall of mirrors as they do in Kesselman's play (Hart 1989; Coffman 1999). The characters are filmed in such a way that their physical positions often mirror each other. The sisters reflect each other and are indeed presented as 'âmes siamoises' to use Lacan's phrase. The same can be said of the mother and daughter, most notably in the scene where they are looking into the mirror and are described by Madame as a 'pair'. Mother and daughter here are operating as sisters. This is mirrored in the photograph of them which is given to the daughter by the mother, which in turn is mirrored by the photograph that the girls have taken of themselves (the photographer asks if they are twins). Not only do mother and daughter become sisters, but by a similar inversion the elder sister frequently plays mother to the younger sister's child reflecting the mother–daughter relationship of the employers. This is often brought out in the brushing of hair as in the first scene.

At the same time it can also be said, as Cixous observes in *La Jeune née* (1975), that the maid is the repressed of the mistress of the house. The open sexuality between the sisters is repressed in the relationship which exists between mother and daughter. This is particularly evident when a card game between mother and daughter below stairs is interspersed by scenes depicting the lovemaking of the sisters above stairs (above and below stairs being the inverse of what they signify in England). The climax for mother and daughter occurs when Madame wins the game.

Both mother and daughter constantly strive to keep all feeling tightly under control when in each other's presence. This is made clear by the fact that Isabelle guzzles chocolates and dances when her mother is not around. Similarly, Madame dances to light music but replaces it with a solemn piece as soon as her daughter appears. The strict time marked by the metronome as they play a duet together also highlights the way in which passion is kept tightly under wraps. Madame's obsession with checking the sisters' work and running her hands over the furniture with white gloves (an aspect common to many employers' behaviour at the time as Beauvoir in her piece on the Papin sisters notes) also highlights her repressed sexuality. Interestingly, it is Madame's thoroughness which Christine appreciates saying: 'Madame knows her place. She checks everything.' Initially the sisters also know their place which is equally appreciated by Madame. It is when the sisters stop knowing their place and do not act in accordance with it that the relationship between the two couples begins to break down and it is really only a matter of time before the situation comes to a head. This is made clear by the use of the dripping tap which appears more and more frequently throughout the film marking the inexorability of time passing and the deterioration of relations.

As in the real-life story, the ending is precipitated by the iron blowing its fuse and plunging the upper floors of the house into darkness. Having burnt Isabelle's blouse (in *My Sister in this House* it is Madame Danzard's blouse which is burnt), Lea and Christine retire to their room and await the return of their mistresses. The latter come back to a dark house, a broken glass in the sink, and the maids nowhere to be seen. Madame makes her way to the first landing, followed by a reluctant Isabelle and is greeted by a dishevelled Christine holding a candle. What follows is as much Madame's loss of control as it is the sisters' violence. In fact, Madame's behaviour and language deteriorate first. She accuses Christine of being a liar and when the latter says that she and her sister will leave, Madame is adamant that they will never find another household prepared to take them in, not after what she has *seen* (and this reminds us of Dupré's point that it must have been an 'observation' on the part of Madame Lancelin which brought about the *transfert maternel* in the first place). When Christine says Madame has seen nothing Madame replies: 'Nothing? Nothing? That hair! That face! You smell of it my dear. (It is at this point that Christine is joined by the terrified Lea.) Just look at that sister of yours. You'll never work with her again. God forgive me for what I have harboured here! You dirt! You scum! Scum sisters.' This is accompanied by her spitting into the sisters' faces. Her screaming and spitting unleash feelings which have been long repressed and are essentially an oral ejaculation. As Michele Aaron points out: 'Whose orgasm is displaced in the murder? Are not all four women implicated in the explosive release of sexual frustration? Indeed, are not Mme and Mlle the most frustrated pair?' (Aaron 1999: 79).

For Christine and Lea, the murders resolve conflicts which were clearly established in childhood. In asserting that Christine and her sister will never work together again, Madame falls into the place of the mother figure who separates the sisters and the castrating father figure who intends to disrupt the unity of mother and child. The solution here is to destroy the bad mother of mother-Madame and castrate the castrator by tearing out the eyes of father-Madame to preserve the unity of both the sister–sister and the mother–Christine, daughter–Lea dyad. Just as Madame defaces and ejaculates by spitting out words and then saliva, the sisters climax by plucking out the eyes and hacking into the younger woman's buttocks and calves with a kitchen knife.

The murder is also a response to what Madame claims that she has 'seen', just as the murder in Chabrol's film is the indirect result of what Melinda 'sees' when she assumes Sophie's fake spectacles and understands that she is dyslexic. When Christine replies that Madame has seen nothing, we recall her earlier remark to her sister that: '[Madame] sees things, things that aren't even there, her and her daughter.' She is, as Lacan would have it, paranoid. In plucking out her mistresses' eyes, she is in true Oedipal fashion punishing herself, that mirror of herself which reflects back to her the truth of her relationship with her sister: that it is sexual and incestuous. The film therefore seems to rest on a paradox: on the one hand, it makes the sexual and incestuous relationship between the sisters very evident (thus undermining Lacan's premiss), on the other hand, the ending suggests that this relationship is something which the sisters are unable consciously to confront. There is also a sense in which unless their relationship is named as such (which it never is) it does not exist.

Sister my Sister is also equally ambivalent when it comes to portraying lesbian sexuality. On the one hand, it privileges relationships between women, in that the film is more or less devoid of men and the only sexuality portrayed is that between women, repressed or otherwise. On the other, it suggests that lesbian relationships cannot be anything other than deviant. This becomes more and more evident as the film progresses. After the sisters return to the house one day, Madame remarks on their appearance to Isabelle: 'They don't even look like maids anymore. They're losing their looks my dear. Have you noticed how thin they've become? And those circles under the eyes. It's as if they never sleep.' What is emerging here is a picture of a destructive sexuality which makes its subject a victim. We are reverting to a discourse which the film seemed initially to be trying to undermine. For the picture which is beginning to develop is that of the lesbian vampire which, by the time of the 'splatter' scene, has become full blown. The Christine who emerges from her attic room, lit only by the candle she is carrying and who meets Madame on the landing, is an unmistakable vampire figure. The blood which the sisters draw in the murders can therefore be construed as the vampires drinking their fill of human blood.

A similar ambiguity lies at the level of language. As in Chabrol's film, language is something which remains essentially a tool of power, akin to the gaze. The silence which exists between mistresses and maids in Meckler is offset by the mindless chatter and gossip of the mistresses when the maids are not present. Language as a form of power and as a constructive tool evades the women in a way that it does not evade men. In the end the sisters are brought under control and judged by a male voice and a male gaze. The final sequences which retrace the aftermath of the murders from the bottom of the stairs to the top, thereby reversing the opening scenes, are accompanied by the voice-over of the magistrates at the trial. During the questioning the sisters remain silent. The voice-over eventually coincides with the last image of the film which is of the two sisters naked and huddled together in bed—fixed, it is implied, by the gaze of the male police officer.

This final image, which becomes a freeze frame, assumes the role of the 'after' pictures of the Papin sisters which were taken by the police and were subsequently reproduced in the press and by the Surrealists. The implication is that they do not look as they do as a result of the killings, as many readings, from the Surrealists to Sartre to Beauvoir suggest, but because of their sexuality, especially because the magistrates' questions dwell not on the murders but on the nature of their relationship. What is of consequence therefore is not so much the violence of the killings, but the nature of the sisters' sexuality, and it is this which the male powers seek to bring under control. On the one hand, they succeed, the women are frozen in the final image and the sound of the cell door locking is heard. However, the last sound which is heard is Christine crying out Lea's name. This conflicts with the final message which appears on the screen telling us what happened to the sisters and which states Christine never spoke her sister's name again. What remains with us is the acoustic image, rather than the written one. The film therefore suggests that although the sisters may have been brought under control in a physical sense, the force of their passion could not be quelled by the male discourse surrounding the trial and which, for many years, dominated its interpretation.

Conclusion

The number, complexity, and variety of the texts with which we have been dealing here—from contemporary daily journalism to psychoanalytic theory, from classics of the French theatre and cinema to popular novelistic recreations—not only makes this an ideal case for looking at in a cultural studies perspective but of itself suggests the ultimate futility of seeking anything so reductive as an 'explanation' of the Papin sisters' crime. What we hope to have achieved is rather a purchase on its extraordinary, and continuing, fascination, which stems from, as it leads back to, many of the key topoi of contemporary French culture. The gulf between Paris and *la France profonde*, the persistence of elements of a feudal class system well into the bourgeois twentieth century, the themes of deviance and criminality, most insistently of all perhaps the importance of the Other and of mirroring—these have recurred throughout our study, and in their overdetermined overlapping cast troubling and iridescent light upon an act that solicits clarification as insistently as it refuses it.

Murder is nowadays big publishing business. Any railway station or airport bookstall will provide evidence of the burgeoning contemporary interest in it, above all in serial killing, which now appears to have been the defining crime of the last days of the twentieth century. The Papin case is strange among other things because it is at the antipodes of the serial killing, and of the wide open postmodern social and ethical spaces that are its concomitants. Serial killing is by definition metonymic; each killing makes sense only in so far as it takes its place in the series and its signifying chain of desire. The Papins, from the heart of their agoraphobia, killed once and once only—it would be impossible to imagine a repetition—with a passionate fervour that makes that killing the ultimate metaphorical crime. The opposition of metaphor and metonymy was formulated by the linguist Roman Jakobson and forms an important part of Lacan's structuring of the unconscious like a language. Malcolm Bowie succinctly explains that 'metaphor is "one word for another" and metonymy a matter of "word to word" connections within the signifying chain' (Bowie 1991: 68). Metaphor thus tends to be associated with identity and fusion, not to say with necessity—thus to be somewhat out of place in a postmodern theoretical landscape dominated by deferral, difference, contingency. This is why it has not exactly had a good press in contemporary critical theory, where it has tended to be seen as reductive, stressing what texts mean rather than how they mean. From Saussure's early view of language as a chain of signifying differences, through Lacan's privileging of the metonymic axis via his deployment of the symbolic, to the anti-referential tendency of virtually all postmodernism, metaphor has been the bridesmaid and metonymy the sophisticatedly blushing bride. One major exception to this is, paradoxically in view of what has just been said, Slavoj Žižek's version of Jacques Lacan, with 'his thesis that metonymic sliding must always be supported by a metaphorical cut' (Žižek 1989: 154). Another is Julia Kristeva, who in *Histoires d'amour* reinscribes the 'objet métaphorique de l'amour' against the 'objet métonymique du désir'[1] (Kristeva 1983: 44).

As we have seen, the Papins' tale was among other things a story of love for each other—a love at once so engulfing and so inarticulate that its possible frustration and interruption could issue only in 'les métaphores les plus usées de la haine', to reprise Lacan. The ferocity of their attack represented a demonic fusion, a destruction of difference through a killing of the not-self/Other that was at the same time a killing of self, which was perhaps—if such a thing be possible—the metaphorical in its pure state. That metaphor, through all the attempts to understand and conceptualize the crime, has remained collapsed in upon itself like a black hole (like the black holes that Madame Lancelin and Geneviève were left with in lieu of eyes?). Georges Oubert wrote in *Paris-Soir* (1 Oct. 1933) that for most people to whom he had spoken in Le Mans: 'Il y a autre chose, dit-on. L'énigme demeure entière.'[2] Through its multiple mirrorings, as well as in spite of them, this has remained obstinately true of any attempt to speak—to see—the truth of the dreadful silent eloquence of Christine and Léa Papin's act.

---

[1] 'the metaphorical object of love . . . the metonymic object of desire.'

[2] 'There is something else, people say. The enigma is still unresolved.' The 'dit-on' may remind us of Dupré's formulation about the ' "on-dit" des soeurs Papin dans le frayage de la psychanalyse'.

Afterword

This book was about to go to press when we heard from Paris that the Papin affair had made a spectacular return to public attention in France. Two films, both produced by the same company (ARP), were released at the end of 2000—a fictional reconstruction of the crime and the events leading up to it (*Les Blessures assassines/Murderous Wounds*, directed by Jean-Pierre Denis), and a documentary inquiry into the crime and its aftermath (*En quête des soeurs Papin/In Search of the Papin Sisters*, directed by Claude Ventura).

More or less simultaneously, two new books on the sisters were published. Sophie Darblade-Mamouni's *L'Affaire Papin* is a fairly straightforward retelling of the affair, with some new contextual information, while Gérard Gourmel's *L'Ombre double: dits et non dits de l'affaire Papin/The Double Shadow: The Said and the Unsaid in the Papin Affair* casts serious doubt upon the reliability of official accounts and the thoroughness of the trial. Why the case should have returned to prominence at precisely this time it is difficult to say. Michèle Halberstadt, of the ARP production company, suggested to Denis (who had not directed a cinema film for twelve years and had been forced to return to his former profession working for the French equivalent of Customs and Excise) that he use Paulette Houdyer's book as the basis for a screenplay. There had earlier been talk of a film to be directed by Maurice Pialat, a much better-known director but one whose temperamental awkwardness was legendary, but that came to nothing.

In tandem with the fictional reconstruction, ARP commissioned from Claude Ventura, best known for his work on the weekly television programme *Cinéma, cinémas*, his documentary. Ventura declared in an interview between the two directors: '[T]u cherchais la vérité avec des acteurs, moi je cherchais la fiction avec des témoins'[1] (*Le Monde*, 22 November 2000)—a succinct distillation of the divergences and convergences between reconstruction and investigation, which the two films bring stimulatingly into focus. The fact that, unusually, there were two films drew much attention to them, and Gourmel's book at least was clearly inspired by this. His description of the affair as 'un témoin de

---

[1] 'You were looking for truth with actors, I was looking for fiction with witnesses.'

l'histoire des mentalités'[2] (Gourmel 2000: 8) suggests how his approach might overlap with that adopted here.

Denis's film deals not at all with the trial or the aftermath of the case, though the murder was filmed, apparently over five days, in gory detail. It is distinguished by outstanding performances from the two young actresses, Sylvie Testud (Christine) and Julie-Marie Parmentier (Léa), whose not-quite-stardom earned them much laudatory critical attention. Sylvie Testud claims to have emancipated herself from Christine's influence after filming finished by not speaking for a month— whether strictly true or not, a highly apposite way of dealing with what must have been a very traumatic role. *Les Blessures assassines* belongs to what might be called the 'French provincial film'—a kind of sub-genre of the heritage movie that numbers such diverse works as Berri's *Jean de Florette* and Assayas's *Les Destinées sentimentales*—giving a careful period reconstruction in which the physical drudgery of the sisters' existence and the lumbering tedium of life in 1930s Le Mans are convincingly evoked. The role of objects is stressed, notably in a powerful scene in which Christine plays more and more violently with an iron rim she has detached from one of the kitchen hot plates, throwing it repeatedly to the floor. Reviews were on the whole favourable, fascinated by the 'pouvoir disruptif d'une folie en germe'[3] (Joyard 2000: 79) and by how this illustrates that '[a]insi donc se construit aussi l'imaginaire collectif d'un pays'[4] (Lorian 2000).

For students of the Papin case, as opposed to those of cinema, it is however Ventura's documentary that is likely to prove the more interesting—this, in spite of its obtrusive use of *noir*esque music (by Miklos Rosza, a leading Hollywood composer for such as Billy Wilder) and heavily atmospheric style, which led *Le Monde* to contrast it unfavourably with *Les Blessures assassines* ('Aussi racoleur que l'autre est sobre, aussi inutile que l'autre paraît essentiel'[5]—22 November 2000). Maybe so; but the final sequence of *En quête des soeurs Papin* is a bombshell for anybody (such as the present authors) who knows, or thought they knew, the details of the affair. The lengthy reconstruction carried out, for the camera and in voice-over, by Pascale Thirode throws up more and more suggestions that documents pertaining to the case were at some time tampered with. M. Lancelin is revealed to have been embroiled in a major financial scandal involving many senior figures of

---

[2] 'A testimony to the history of ways of thinking.'
[3] '[The] disruptive power of a germinating madness.'
[4] 'This is how the collective imaginary of a country is constructed.'
[5] 'As over-emphatic as the other film is sober, as pointless as the other seems essential.'

the business community in Le Mans (then as now a major insurance centre), and there is a hint that Christine might at some time have used the word 'escroc'/crook in alluding to him. The death of the eldest sister, Émilia, hitherto 'missing without trace', is recorded as having taken place in the small Breton town of Pontivy in 1986, but no comparable record exists for Léa. Ventura and Thirard's inquiries take them to Nantes, where it turns out Léa had been living under her own name until very recently. Neighbours, evidently unaware of her 'true' identity, obligingly describe her as a delightful little old lady who 'trotted around' cheerfully, loved looking after children, and never missed an episode of the television programme *Les Feux de l'amour/The Fires of Love*.

And so to the final sequence, in which the camera climbs up to a room—presumably in some form of hospice—outside which the name of Léa Papin is displayed. Léa had been taken there after suffering a brain haemorrhage which had left her unable to speak, and we finally see her, bedridden, being spoken to affectionately by Pascale Thirode (but how much does she understand?). This sequence provoked much criticism, and Ventura has expressed his own anxieties about its propriety. Léa's words in a statement after her arrest: 'Désormais, je suis sourde et muette'[6] receive an all too literal confirmation, and the audience is left in a deeply uncomfortable voyeuristic position.

The rightness of its dealings with Léa aside, what is extraordinary about Ventura's film is the degree of manipulation of the facts and official records of the case it brings to light. This is amply borne out by Gourmel's book, which goes into juicy detail about the scandal in which the hitherto supposedly irreproachable M. Lancelin was involved and shows how the presentation of material at the trial was increasingly slanted to suggest that Christine was effectively the sole agent of the murders. The 'folie à deux' invoked by Lacan was, it would seem, too much for a provincial assize court to digest. Gourmel provides a meticulous montage of statements from the sisters, press coverage, police accounts, and psychiatrists' reports, all time and again contradicting one another in a manner which shows that however swiftly the trial disposed of the case it certainly did not provide a full or accurate record of what happened on 2 February 1933. Such a record, of course, will now never exist. More clearly than ever now it appears that:

Au long de l'affaire Papin, à chaque noeud du drame, s'inscrivent silences, occultations, demi et contre-vérités, manques, irrégularités et doutes.[7]

---

[6] 'From now on, I am deaf and dumb.'
[7] 'All through the Papin affair, at each key point in the drama, we find silences, things concealed, half-truths and untruths, absences, irregularities, and doubts.'

Chronology

Bibliography

Aaron, Michele (1999), ''Til Death Us Do Part: Cinema's Queer Couples Who Kill',
in Michele Aaron (ed.), *The Body's Perilous Pleasures: Dangerous Desires and
Contemporary Culture* (Edinburgh: Edinburgh University Press), 67–84.

Anderson, Benedict (1991), *Imagined Communities*, 2nd edn. (London/New York:
Verso).

Auclair, Georges (1970), *Le Mana quotidien* (Paris: Anthropos).

Austin, Guy (1999), *Claude Chabrol* (Manchester: Manchester University Press).

Balzac, Honoré de (1971), *Le Père Goriot* (Paris: Gallimard).

Bataille, Georges (1970), *Histoire de l'oeil*, œuvres complètes, 1, 1st pub. 1922–40
(Paris: Gallimard).

Beauvoir, Simone de (1960), *La Force de l'âge* (Paris: Gallimard).

Bellemin-Noel, Jean (1986), 'Le Diamant noir: échographie d'*Erostrate*', *Littérature*,
64: 71–89.

Bennington, Geoffrey (1988), *Lyotard: Writing the Event* (Manchester: Manchester
University Press).

Bersani, Leo (1995), *Homos* (Cambridge, Mass., and London: Harvard University
Press).

Berthomieu, Pierre, Jeancolas, Jean-Pierre, and Vassé, Claire (1995), 'Entretien avec
Claude Chabrol', *Positif* (Sept.), 415: 8–14.

Birch, Helen (1994) (ed.), *Moving Targets: Women, Murder and Representation*
(Berkeley and Los Angeles: University of California Press).

Bory, Jean-Louis (1963), '*Les Abysses*: le vertige des ténèbres', *Arts* (17 Apr. 1963).

Bourdieu, Pierre (1979), *La Distinction* (Paris: Minuit).

Bowie, Malcolm (1991), *Lacan* (London: Fontana).

Breton, André (1983), *Manifestes du surréalisme* (Paris: Gallimard).

Cameron, Deborah, and Frazer, Elizabeth (1987), *The Lust to Kill: A Feminist
Investigation of Sexual Murder* (Oxford: Polity Press).

Chadwick, Whitney (1985), *Women Artists and the Surrealist Movement* (London:
Thames and Hudson).

Chaussumier, Jacques (1984), untitled article in *La Vie mancelle*, no. 227.

Coffman, Christine E. (1999), 'The Papin Enigma', *GLQ* 5/3: 331–59.

Constant, Benjamin (1961), *Adolphe* (Manchester: Manchester University Press).

Darblade-Mamouni, S. (2000), *L'Affaire Papin* (Paris: Éditions De Vecchi).

De Bruyn, Olivier (1995), 'Claude Chabrol: maître de cérémonie', *Evénement du
jeudi* (24–30 Aug.).

De Lauretis, Teresa (1998), 'The Stubborn Drive', *Critical Inquiry*, 24: 851–77.

De Man, Paul (1983), *Blindness and Insight* (London: Methuen).

Derrida, Jacques (1967), *L'Écriture et la différence* (Paris: Seuil).

Derrida, Jacques (1974), *Glas* (Paris: Galilée).

Dupré, Francis (1984), *La 'Solution' du passage à l'acte: le double crime des soeurs Papin* (Toulouse: Érès).

Éluard, Paul, and Péret, Benjamin (1933), 'Les Soeurs Papin furent élevées au couvent du Mans', *Le Surréalisme au service de la Révolution*, 5: 27–8.

Fitch, Noel Riley (1985), *Sylvia Beach and the Lost Generation* (Harmondsworth: Penguin).

Flanner, Janet (1972), *Paris Was Yesterday: 1925–1939* (New York: Viking).

Forbes, Jill (1997), *Les Enfants du paradis* (London: British Film Institute).

Foubert-Daudet, Yvonne (1982), *La Règle du je* (Toulouse: Érès).

Foucault, Michel (1982), 'Afterword: The Subject and Power', in Hubert L. Dreyfus and Paul Rabinow (eds.), *Michel Foucault: Beyond Structuralism and Hermeneutics* (Brighton: Harvester).

Freud, Sigmund (1985), 'The Uncanny', in *Art and Literature* (London/New York).

Gauthier, Xavière (1971), *Surréalisme et sexualité* (Paris: Gallimard).

Genet, Jean (1976), *Les Bonnes* (Paris: Gallimard).

Genette, Gérard (1982), *Palimpsestes: la littérature au second degré* (Paris: Seuil).

Gilbert, Sandra M., and Gubar, Susan (1979), *The Madwoman in the Attic: The Woman Writer and the Nineteenth-Century Literary Imagination* (New Haven: Yale University Press).

Godzich, Wlad (1983), 'Caution! Reader at Work!', in Paul de Man, *Blindness and Insight* (London: Methuen).

Gourmel, G. (2000), *L'Ombre double: dits et non dits de l'affaire Papin* (Le Mans: Cénomane).

Guérin, M.-A., and Jousse, T. (1995), 'Entretien avec Claude Chabrol', *Cahiers du cinéma*, 494: 27–35.

Guérin, M.-A., and Taboulay C. (1997), 'La Connivence: entretien avec Isabelle Huppert', *Cahiers du cinéma*, 68.

Hart, Lynda (1989), ' "They don't even look like maids anymore": Wendy Kesselman's *My Sister in this House*', in Lynda Hart (ed.), *Making a Spectacle: Feminist Essays on Contemporary Women's Theatre* (Ann Arbor: University of Michigan Press), 131–46.

——(1994), *Fatal Women: Lesbian Sexuality and the Mark of Aggression* (Princeton: Princeton University Press).

Hayman, Ronald (1986), *Writing Against: A Biography of Sartre* (London: Weidenfeld and Nicolson).

Houdyer, Paulette (1966), 'Il y a trente-trois ans, les "filles" Papin', in *La Vie mancelle*, no. 68.

——(1988), *L'Affaire Papin: le diable dans la peau* (Le Mans: Cénomane).

Hughes, Alex (1998), entry on *écriture féminine* in Alex Hughes and Keith Reader (eds.), *Encyclopedia of Contemporary French Culture* (London and New York: Routledge).

Jones, Ann (1980), *Women Who Kill* (New York: Holt, Rinehart and Winston).

Jousse, T. (1995), 'Cinq motifs pour Claude Chabrol', *Cahiers du cinéma*, 494: 34–5.

Joyard, O. (2000), 'Soeurs de sang', *Cahiers du cinéma*, December.

Kamenish, P. (1996), 'Naming the Crime: Responses to the Papin Murders from Lacan, Beauvoir and Flanner', *The Comparatist: Journal of the Southern Comparative Literature Association*, 20: 93–110.

Kesselman, Wendy (1982), *My Sister in this House* (New York: Samuel French).

Kilkelly, Ann Gavere (1986), 'Who's in the House?', *Women and Performance: A Journal of Feminist Theory*, 5/3: 28–34.

Kristeva, Julia (1983), *Histoires d'amour* (Paris: Gallimard).

Lacan, Jacques (1975*a*), *De la psychose paranoïaque dans ses rapports avec la personnalité suivi de premiers écrits sur la paranoïa* (Paris: Seuil).

—— (1975*b*), *Le Séminaire XX: Encore!* (Paris: Seuil).

Lane, Christopher (1993), ' "The Delirium of Interpretation": Writing the Papin Affair', *Différences: A Journal of Feminist Cultural Studies*, 5/2: 25–61.

Lautréamont, Comte de (1874, 1977), *Les Chants de Maldoror* (Paris: Presses de la Renaissance).

Leak, Andrew (1989), *The Perverted Consciousness: Sexuality and Sartre* (London: Macmillan).

Le Guillant, Louis (1963), 'L'Affaire des soeurs Papin', in *Les Temps modernes*, no. 210.

Lessana, Marie-Magdeleine (2000), *Entre mère et fille: un ravage* (Paris: Pauvert).

Le Texier, Robert (1994), *Les Soeurs Papin* (Paris: Fleuve Noir).

Lorian, F.-G. (2000), review in *Le Point* (18 November).

Macey, David (1988), *Lacan in Contexts* (London and New York: Verso).

Magedera, Ian (1998), *Genet: Les Bonnes* (Glasgow: University of Glasgow French and German Publications).

Merleau-Ponty, Maurice (1960), 'Sur les faits divers', in *Signes* (Paris: Gallimard).

Millett, Kate (1977), *Sexual Politics* (London: Virago).

Nougé, Paul (1933), 'Les Images défendues', *Le Surréalisme au service de la révolution*, 5: 24–8.

Positif (1988), 451: 57.

Powrie, Phil (1997), *French Cinema in the 1980s: Nostalgia and the Crisis of Masculinity* (Oxford and New York: Oxford University Press).

Rendell, Ruth (1994), *A Judgement in Stone*, 2nd edn. (London: Arrow Books).

Rifkin, Adrian (1993), *Street Noises: Parisian Pleasures 1900–1940* (Manchester and New York: Manchester University Press).

Robillon, Dominique (1981), untitled article in *Cénome* (spring number).

Roudinesco, Élisabeth (1993), *Jacques Lacan* (Paris: Fayard).

Saint-Drôme, Oreste (1994), *Dictionnaire inespéré de 55 termes visités par Jacques Lacan* (Paris: Seuil).

Sartre, Jean-Paul (1939), 'Érostrate', in *Le Mur* (Paris: Gallimard).

—— (1952), *Saint Genet, comédien et martyr* (Paris: Gallimard).

Savona, J.-L. (1983), *Jean Genet* (London: Macmillan).

Sellers, Susan (1994), Preface to *The Hélène Cixous Reader* (London and New York: Routledge).

Strauss, F. (1995), 'Lesdits commandements', *Cahiers du cinéma*, 494: 24–6.

Thody, Philip (1960), *Jean-Paul Sartre* (London: Hamish Hamilton).

Turkle, Sherry (1979), *Psychoanalytic Politics* (London: Burnett Books/André Deutsch).

Ungar, Steven (1998), entry on Jean-Paul Sartre in Alex Hughes and Keith Reader (eds.), *Encyclopedia of Contemporary French Culture* (London and New York: Routledge).

Walker, David (1995), *Outrage and Insight: Modern French Writers and the fait divers* (Oxford and Herndon, USA: Berg).

Ward Jouve, Nicole (1998), 'Maleness in the Act: The Case of the Papin Sisters', in *Female Genesis: Creativity, Self and Gender* (Cambridge: Polity).

White, Edmund (1993), *Genet* (London: Chatto and Windus).

Winock, Michel (1987), *Chronique des années soixante* (Paris: Le Monde/Seuil).

Woodle, Gary (1974), '*Erostrate*: Sartre's Paranoid', *Review of Existential Psychology and Psychiatry*, 13: 30–41.

Žižek, Slavoj (1989), *The Sublime Object of Ideology* (London and New York: Verso).

Index

This includes proper names of individuals, places, and publications, with the exception of fictional characters, Paris, and members of the Papin and Lancelin families, to whom references are too numerous to itemize.